INTRODUCTION TO
HORSERIDING

Contents

Introduction   6

Choosing a School   8

Understanding Horses   18

The First Lesson   28

Equine Movement   42

Technical Improvement   54

Hacking and Jumping   84

Glossary   111

Index   112

Introduction

If you enjoy active sports, or would like to, and you have a love of the countryside, animals and the great outdoors, then horse-riding is for you. People of all ages, shapes and sizes can learn. Physical disabilities need not be a barrier. Learning the basics does not take long and will give you enough knowledge to be able to ride a quiet horse in the company of others. To be a really accomplished rider takes dedication and time, and having got started, there is no limit to how much more you can learn and achieve.

This book is intended as a guide for the novice rider; to help you understand a little more about what makes horses tick, why and how they behave as they do. It is impossible to learn to ride from a book without practical experience, but with an understanding of the basic principles, you should be able to progress much more quickly.

Horseriding can be exhilarating or relaxing, dangerous or just fun, depending on what you want to get out of it. Either way, it is certainly challenging and opens up all kinds of possibilities to the enthusiast. Whether you want to jog along a beach on holiday, trek across some part of the world that would otherwise be inaccessible by any other means of transport, or just meet with new people sharing a common interest, I hope this book will help you. Horses have enriched the lives of millions of people through the ages, capturing the imagination and stretching both mind and body to the limit. So, welcome to the world of horses and horseriding. If you only get half the pleasure from your new activity that I have from a lifetime with horses, you have some wonderful times ahead of you.

Choosing a School

Choosing the right school is of vital importance. If you are badly or inappropriately taught at the beginning, it can be extremely difficult to correct faults later on. The first step is to get a list of riding schools within reasonable traveling distance from home.

Find out whether they are approved by a national body and subject to regular inspections. If so, then the chances are that the teaching methods used will be basically sound and that the horses and buildings will be well looked after. Riding is, after all, a risky sport and sloppy management will invariably lead to a higher accident rate. Make an appointment to visit any possible centers before making a booking. This will give you a chance to compare one with another and see for yourself whether the place suits your needs.

Making a list of questions to ask on your first visit will ensure that nothing is overlooked. This is obviously personal. Each school will have its own particular strengths and specialities to be taken into account. For example, if you want a course of basic lessons to set you up for a riding holiday, then an opportunity to ride out in the

LEFT: *Contented horses in well-built and ventilated stables.*

BELOW LEFT: *An indoor lesson with riders being coached in the basic jumping position. This is a safe riding environment giving the best possible opportunity for learning.*

RIGHT: *A clean and busy yard. It is obvious that a high standard of care is being maintained here.*

BELOW: *A chance to ride in open countryside on well-behaved horses is the ideal way to learn by experience. The horses will tend to stick together while the rider has a chance to get used to the feel of the horses' movement.*

countryside will be near the top of your list. On the other hand, if you fancy learning about dressage and would really like to become a skilful rider, then an indoor riding arena is going to be more important than open fields. It is much easier for both rider and horse to concentrate indoors, and does mean that bad weather is no longer an inhibiting factor. However, some points should be raised regardless of the type of riding you would like to concentrate on.

Safety for the rider should come first. Does the school insist on safe headgear, at least for novices? Does it insist on a particular style of footwear and other clothing? There is no sense in being brave and foolish, so a well-run school should insist on certain standards. We have all seen pictures of riders galloping along a beach, hair flowing behind them and feet bare, but this comes later (perhaps!) if you want to take risks on your own. Find out if you are allowed to choose your own horse to ride or if your instructor-to-be prefers to choose for you. The latter is preferable. He (or she) should have the option of matching the horses he knows best to the riders' size and ability. These are points which can be raised over the telephone and could possibly save a wasted journey.

Welfare of the horses comes next on the list. This is best judged by visiting the school to see for yourself. The number of hours a horse is allowed to work each week is almost irrelevant as their needs vary. The important factor is that they can be seen to be able to cope with their

work. Look at the overall impression the horses give. They should all be taking an interest in their surroundings, though obviously not all will be in a good mood at the same time. Alert expressions, ears flicking back and forth, heads turning to observe people moving around, are all signs of good health. Should all the horses be standing with heads down, ears back and eyes half-closed, then the chances are that they may be either overworked or underfed or both.

Fit horses may have their ribs showing, but this level of fitness is only normally to be seen in competition horses, particularly if they do fast work. Racehorses are obvious examples – they are kept as light as possible and carry a great deal of muscle rather than fat. A riding school full of 'ribby' horses is below par and should be avoided. A healthy horse in steady work should look rounded rather than angular, with a glossy coat and healthy skin. Any sign of dullness, sores or unsoundness is not good, particularly where it applies to the majority of animals rather than the minority. At any one time there is a chance that one or two horses may be off color, or difficult to keep in good condition. It is the general impression which counts. Even so, a lame horse should not be in work at any time.

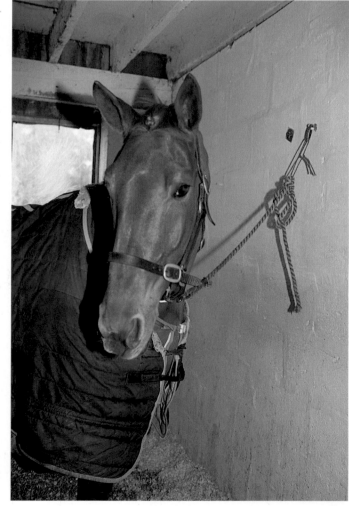

ABOVE: *Jenny Loriston-Clarke riding 'Dutch Bid' in a dressage class at Hickstead. Dressage epitomizes the peak of achievement in the training of horse and rider.*

LEFT: *A horse tied up correctly and safely, using a quick release knot. The rope is threaded through a loop of string which will break if the horse panics.*

ABOVE RIGHT: *Lusitano stallions on pillar reins in Portugal. All these horses are glowing with health – clearly well-fed, exercised, and cared for.*

RIGHT: *Ground feeding. Well-fed horses are less likely to fight than their hungry counterparts.*

Cleanliness is also part of good management. Horses can be difficult to keep clean – they produce a lot of manure, like to roll in mud or dust and (particularly in a cooler climate) make a lot of grease in the coat as natural weather proofing. Without regular grooming in some form, a horse will be prone to saddle sores, especially if dried mud or dirt is left under the saddle or bridle. Some dirt on the legs is not necessarily a sign of neglect, but, again, if all the horses look ill-kempt, beware. A spotlessly clean and sparkling stable yard sporting a lot of white paint and tubs of flowers is unlikely to house neglected horses, although in some cases, money is spent on appearances while safety and welfare are overlooked. Very often an untidy but basically clean yard contains much-loved and well-cared for horses, as time spent is maintaining high levels of teaching rather than maintaining a cosmetic appearance. In short, try to look below the surface and do not be fooled by outward appearances.

If possible watch a lesson taking place, to get an idea of whether or not you would like to join in. The instructor's approach makes a great difference. Riding should be enjoyable while the instructor remains firmly in control. The sergeant major image is still alive and well, with

LEFT: Young riders with their instructor. Lining up the ponies while the tack is checked and adjusted presents a useful picture for the would-be pupil.

ABOVE: A good roll is nature's way of grooming – it's healthy and it's fun! This is a Caspian pony, a breed which was almost extinct until recently.

many people still believing that shouting is the best way to teach. It is not. If you take lessons then presumably you will make an effort and do not wish to be demoralized. However, it is important that riders and horses all do as they are told to avoid accidents; if people are milling about aimlessly and bumping into one another, then something is amiss.

Good discipline on a lesson will ensure that everybody gets a fair share of instruction and that the horses behave themselves, but it should not be taken to the point where the lesson becomes too military. A very young instructor might struggle to keep a class of adults occupied and learning, but could be marvelous with children. Either way, it is important to feel comfortable with your instructor so that you can progress as well as possible.

Very large groups make learning difficult. A bit of mental arithmetic will tell you how much individual attention to expect on an hour's lesson. Groups of four to eight or perhaps ten are large enough – more than this and the risk factor increases. How much you can afford to pay will have to be considered, but if a cheap lesson means being one of twenty, then you will be much better off paying twice as much to be in a smaller class. Larger groups for riding out are

fine if the horses behave well and there is a sufficient number of experienced riders to help the beginners. Having said that, it is still not a good idea to ride out before having some basic lessons.

If you get the opportunity, wander round the stables and riding area. Do the stables look safe, weatherproof and well-ventilated? Is there provision for the horses to lie down and rest if they are stabled for more than short periods? Are any tethered horses or ponies provided with water, shade and shelter and are they safely tied where there is nothing obvious on which to injure themselves? Would you feel safe riding at this place or are you likely to get strung up on barbed wire or tossed through an unprotected window if the horse misbehaves? Are the riding facilities so poor that novices have to be escorted out on a busy road or along perilous cliff paths before mastering the basics?

Nowhere is perfect. The important thing is that you feel that the instructors will look after your safety, care for the horses, give you a chance to learn properly and that you can enjoy your course of lessons. Horsey people are nearly always friendly and sociable, so that once you are settled in to a place and have made new friends, you will be unlikely to change. This is all the more reason to take care over your initial choice.

PROTECTIVE CLOTHING

Many riding centers have suitable hats available for hire to novices. Although it is far more satisfactory to have your own hat, these are not cheap. Unless you have already done a bit of riding and are quite sure that you are committed, a few trial lessons first will make sure that you really want to continue before parting with the extra cash. The style of hat worn by jockeys offers the best protection. They are quite comfortable, light and easy to fit. You can choose from various colored silk or velveteen covers to suit your taste, as these hats are not particularly flattering on their own. Most tack shops and saddlery outlets stock a range of hats and other riding clothes.

To avoid your feet getting caught in the stirrups, safe footwear is just as important. Avoid any kind of high heel although some kind of heel is necessary to prevent your feet going through the stirrups. Trainers, therefore are not suitable. Ankle protection avoids bruising but a boot with a heavily treaded sole is not advisable. Either short leather riding boots or knee-length rubber or leather riding boots will be the best option once you have decided that riding horses is for you. They are not necessarily expensive and will

last for a long time as well as being comfortable.

Stirrup leathers can pinch and rub the inside of your knees until you are fit, so trousers with a reinforced knee patch (jodhpurs) are a good idea. They are available now in a wide variety of styles and materials including denim and corduroy – a far cry from the original heavy, baggy jodhpurs worn until the 1960s.

During hot weather, although it may seem appealing to pick up a bit of a tan while riding out, some kind of shoulder covering will protect your skin should you fall off. The point of the shoulder is particularly vulnerable so a short sleeved shirt is better than a singlet or sun-top. Blistered hands are another trap for the unfit and inexperienced, so a pair of gloves which will not slip on the reins are a wise (but not essential) investment. Again, enquire at a tack shop. It is possible to spend a lot of money on riding clothes if you are really enthusiastic, but it is better to build up your wardrobe gradually rather than splash out at the beginning. This way you will be sure of getting the right equipment for your type of riding and can take advice from the people you ride with.

BELOW LEFT: *Jodhpurs, knee-high riding boots and a hard hat make riding safer and more comfortable. Reflective clothing for riding on any road, day or night, makes drivers more aware that a horse is a hazard. However, a hat with a chinstrap is safer than the one shown here.*

BELOW: *Between classes at a Pony Club hunter trial. For this sort of activity, a sweater is more practical than a jacket.*

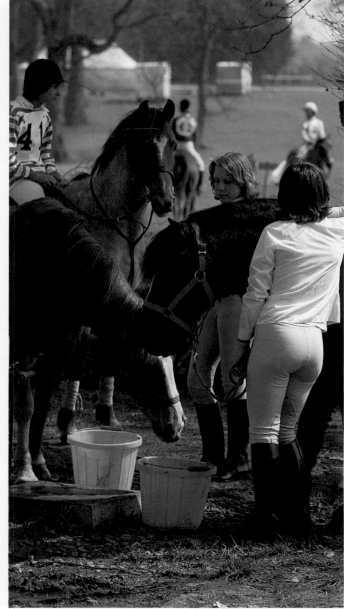

RIGHT: *A day at the races. Professional jockeys wear skull hats which offer the best protection for riders. Note the condition of these horses. They carry more muscle than fat and are clearly very healthy.*

BELOW: *There is no need to sacrifice safety when riding for fun. Riding a native Lusitano along a Portuguese beach is no less attractive for the use of safe tack and clothing.*

Understanding Horses

In comparison with other species horses are not particularly intelligent animals, but they are remarkably sensitive. They are very quick to notice if the person approaching them is nervous, and depending on their own self-esteem, will respond either by taking advantage or becoming nervous themselves. By making a brief study of how horses live in their natural environment, it becomes much easier to understand them and therefore handle them successfully right from the start.

As with other herd animals, horses rely on their numbers, alertness and speed for survival. It is unnatural for a horse to be isolated and this will generally make him much more jumpy. With his head down to graze, a horse can see all round him as his eyes are set wide on the head. Horses' ears tend to flick back and forth indicating in which direction his attention is taken. If the alarm is raised, a herd will run en masse. Although not as quick over short distances as many natural predators (wolves, or big cats for example), speed can be maintained over remarkably long distances.

The individual senses of sight, hearing, smell and touch are very sharp. With this in mind, it is wise to approach a horse quietly, speaking softly and making quite sure that he can see you coming. A predator would approach from the rear, so if caught unawares, a horse will

ABOVE: *A mixed group of horses free to socialize. Note the expression of the dark gray mare with the young foal. She is defensive while taking her foal away from the more dominant and aggressive white-gray mare behind her.*

LEFT: *Watching, listening, alert. Even in this equine paradise a lone horse's attention is easily caught by unusual sounds or movements.*

ABOVE RIGHT: *Youngsters enjoying some mutual grooming. Horses often curl or twist the top lip when relishing a good scratch.*

RIGHT: *This sensible approach reassures a potentially jumpy horse whose attention is not on his handler.*

often kick in self-defense. Avoid simulating this by walking straight up behind a horse which does not know you are there. The muzzle area, particularly via the whiskers is very sensitive. Extending a hand forward so that the horse can nuzzle if he wishes, or just sniff you out is better than launching in with a hearty slap on the neck.

There are two blind spots to be avoided. One is directly behind the hind feet and the other is between the eyes, so avoid trying to pat him anywhere on the front of his face. A horse will only accept this if he has great trust in the handler; as a stranger you will only make him anxious if you try to do it. The normal reaction from the horse is to toss his head upwards, and by standing too close you risk receiving a black eye. While the horse is investigating one hand, move toward his shoulder and, with the other hand, stroke or pat him firmly but gently on the neck just in front of the shoulder. This imitates the mutual grooming that horses enjoy among themselves, and will therefore inspire trust. Horses have ticklish spots, generally along the line of the mane, around the withers (top of the shoulder), and sometimes behind the ears. They appreciate a good scratch, and this is helpful in making friends with your horse; don't be surprised if he tries to nibble you in response to this mutual grooming stimulus. Although it is a friendly gesture on his part, it is not to be encouraged.

LEFT: *With wide-set eyes, horses have excellent all round vision. Ears flicking back and forth while grazing may be the only indication than an apparently relaxed animal is in fact, constantly on the look-out, even during feed times.*

ABOVE: *Even in a small group, turns are taken at drinking. Horses love to drink from as large a volume of water as possible and enjoy a certain amount of water-play during hot weather.*

RIGHT: *The young horse nearest the camera is dominant. He is pushing into the others with his ears back and eyes part-closed.*

Grass is the natural food of the horse. Having low nutritional value, it needs to be eaten in large quantities to provide sufficient nourishment. This means that horses think they need to spend most of their waking hours eating. For a novice rider it can be frustrating to have your mount constantly snatching at mouthfuls of grass or hedgerow instead of concentrating on what he should be doing. If he gets left behind other horses in the group, he will invariably catch them up, only to repeat the action. As your riding improves, the horse will quickly learn to recognize your authority and this annoying tendency will be forgotten.

In a herd situation, there is a distinct hierarchy. This is sometimes demonstrated among domestic horses in a field at drinking time if, for example, the water supply is at the opposite end to where the herd is grazing. The most dominant horse, usually a mare, decides when to move and will take the first drink while the others wait in turn. Until the pecking order is established, there is often a fair amount of squabbling, especially if two horses feel that they should each have the same rank. Some horses are naturally domineering while others are happier keeping out of trouble and will always back off. This is why it is important to be firm in your handling so that you gain a position as a 'herd leader' rather than follower. Using pain or rough handling is not a good idea as this only makes them nervous and ultimately more difficult to handle. If a horse feels

that he has a stronger character than you, he will persistently try to take advantage of this. Attitude of mind is more important than skill alone. A good motto is 'think positive' — it is remarkably effective.

Horses have a variety of ways of expressing their moods and conveying messages. Ears are particularly worth watching. If they are both pointing straight forward, with the head up and nostrils flared, perhaps with the whites of the eyes showing as well, then the horse's alarm bells are jangling. The cause could be something trivial like a distant rustling paper bag, or possibly he can hear or see something which frightens him. Whatever it is, he is certainly not heeding his handler and will need to have his attention brought back before being asked to perform a specific task.

At the opposite end of the scale, ears laid flat back in the mane, nostrils wrinkled and mouth open, is a strong sign of aggression. A dominant

horse doing this to a weaker will require no further action — it is threat enough in itself. If the offending party does not back down, then the aggressor will dart forward and bite. Some horses pull this face frequently when being groomed or having the girth tightened without following up the threat. It is a threat nonetheless, and should be taken seriously if you don't know the horse.

If the ears are flicking alternately back and forth, then the horse is usually calm but listening. If this is accompanied by fidgeting then the horse may be anxious. The expression in his eyes will tell you more. If his gaze is steady and the eye expression is soft, then he is probably calm and alert. A bored horse will lack expression. His ears will be still and partially laid-back with eyes partly closed. Always look your horse in the eye when you approach him. If he returns your gaze and brings his ears gently forward, then he is probably pleased to see you.

In both these pictures, the horses are in no doubt that there is food on the way, and they will be able to see for themselves when the supply has dried up.

By taking a small handful of food from a bucket and offering this on the palm of the hand (see left) it is possible to approach even a nervous horse. This is a good technique to develop which will then be used time and time again. If all the horses on a yard are fed at the same time and in the same order, much of the trauma of feeding time is reduced and the whole process is less hazardous for both handler and horse.

BELOW: *When feeding out of doors, avoid the corners of a paddock as this can lead to cornering and a potentially dangerous situation for the handler. This horse is being very polite and respectful of his young attendant. Whatever the situation this is how a horse should behave.*

It is nice to be able to reward your horse at the end of a ride with a snack. This can, however, lead to biting and other annoying habits. As long as you can continue to feed him when you see him, the horse will be quite happy – it is when you do not have anything for him that the problem arises. He could start by just sniffing your pockets and end up by tearing your clothes or biting in frustration and annoyance. Always check with your instructor before giving rewards, as there may be some regular system at the stable.

If snack feeding is allowed, then get carrots, apples or something similar rather than lumps of sugar or sweets. Offer it on the palm of your hand so that your whole hand, including the thumb is flat. This avoids bitten fingers. Remember that trying to feed one horse in the presence of others is upsetting for the remainder and if they are loose in a paddock they will almost invariably start fighting.

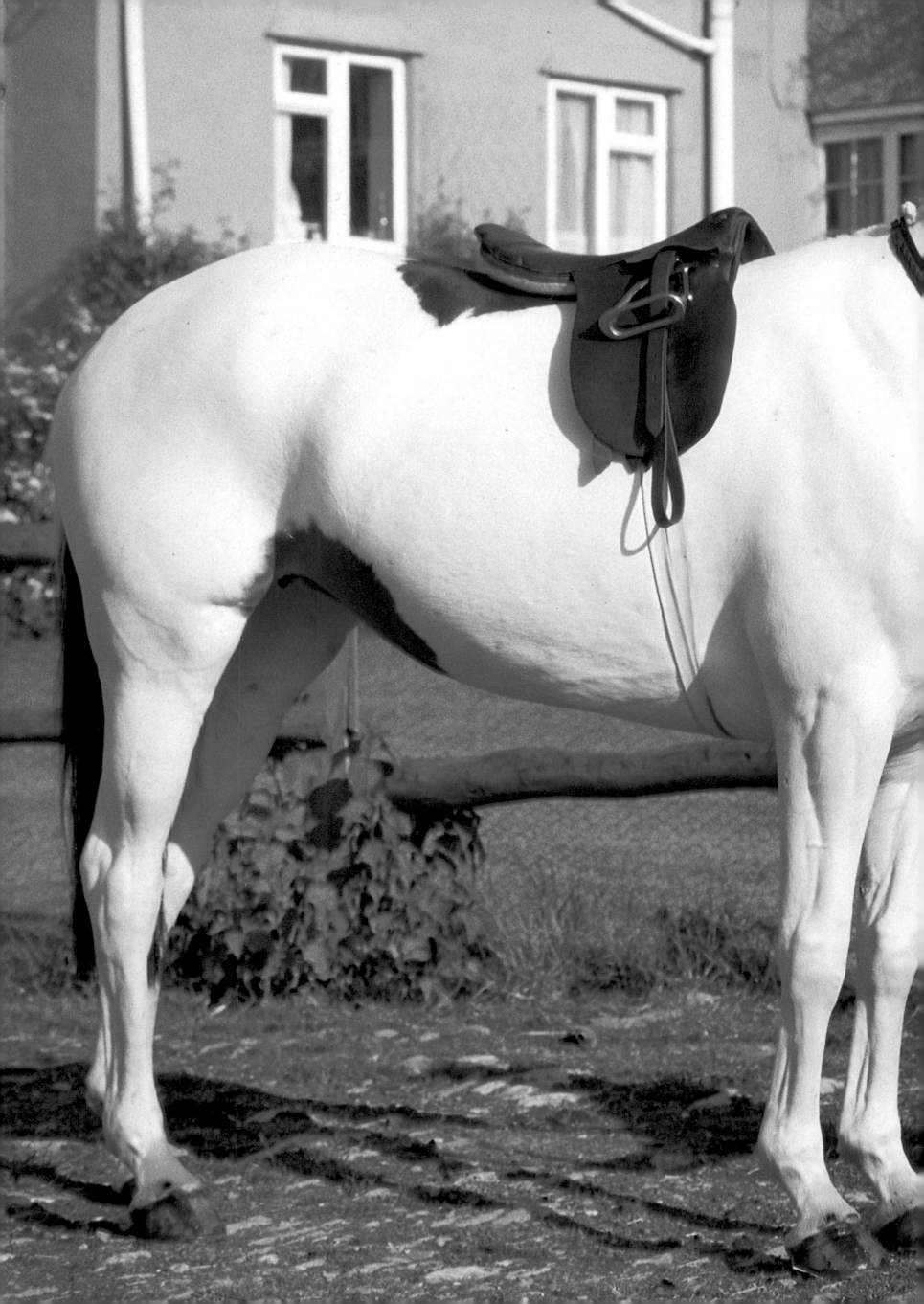

The First Lesson

The best way to lead a horse is to walk on his left side, close to his shoulder. Holding both reins in both hands, place your right hand about 18 inches from his chin with your left hand supporting the spare leather; do not wind it around your hand. This is the safest and most controlled way to lead a horse.

Walking in front of the horse either means that you can't see what he's doing, or you will be looking him straight in the face. The latter will tend to make him back off. Staying by his shoulder has the added advantage of protecting your feet – horses have a nasty habit of treading on toes, even though they will do almost anything to avoid trampling on a rider who has fallen off or tripped over. Presumably, this is because their hooves have almost completely straight sides and their natural instincts do not allow for horizontal human feet.

RIGHT: *How not to lead a horse. The horse's expression shows his unwillingness to go forward.*

BELOW: *With the leader in a better position, the horse is completely confident, and willing.*

ABOVE: *When leading along a road, place yourself between the horse and the traffic, so that the hindquarters cannot easily be swung out to an oncoming car. This means leading from the off side to go with traffic driving on the left side of the road.*

RIGHT: *Showing a child's pony on the leading rein.*

EQUIPMENT

For your first few rides, it is not unreasonable to expect someone more experienced to check your horse's equipment for you. If anything is overlooked it is the rider who will suffer the consequences. It only takes a moment to make sure that the bridle is not likely to fall off, that the girth (holding the saddle in place) is tightened, and that the stirrup leathers are approximately the right length for your height.

The importance of checking tack cannot be over-estimated. At a riding school, the bridle, saddle, and stirrup leathers should be checked regularly when they are cleaned. If you spot obviously shoddy repairs or dangling pieces of cotton, mention it to your instructor. If something breaks when you are out riding, you will lose control of the horse at the very least. This may seem unlikely but it does occur in the remoter parts of the world catering to the holiday trade.

SADDLES

Saddles come in an astonishing variety of styles, shapes and sizes. A general purpose jumping or event saddle allows for riding with shorter stirrups. Dressage saddles and western saddles are unsuitable for jumping, and flat pony or show saddles without knee rolls make jumping more difficult than it should be. The saddle shape goes some way to dictating the length of your stirrups.

The saddle is fastened around the horse with the girth. This is tight enough if you can only just fit your hand between it and the horse below the bottom of the saddle. Keep your fingers flat together and slide your hand under the girth following the lie of the hair. Watch out for a crafty nip as most horses dislike having the girth tightened. Having done this, pull both stirrups down and check their length. The easy method is to place the tips of your fingers on the buckle at the top of the leather and place the bottom of the stirrup against your armpit. If the leather is then taut, the length will be about right. With a tall horse it may help to lengthen the nearside leather for mounting.

Lastly, put the reins over the horse's head, making sure there is one each side and they are not crossed under the neck. As before, avoid standing directly in front of the horse to do this, but rather, flip the reins over from the side.

ABOVE: *Cleaning tack need not be a chore. Supple well-maintained leatherwork is a pleasure to handle. A quick wipe-over after each ride will keep it in good condition, although taking the bridle completely apart is necessary for thorough cleaning and to check the stitching for wear and tear.*

RIGHT: *This quarter horse is beautifully turned out in full Western tack. She is in tip-top condition, not too fat, well-muscled and has a glossy coat. The tack is clean and in good order. Note that this horse is ground tied, which is part of the Western horse's basic training. Never leave the reins trailing unless you are absolutely sure that your horse is trained to this method.*

LEFT: *From left to right, dressage saddle, side saddle, general purpose (G.P.) saddle, race exercise saddle, show saddle.*

BELOW LEFT: *Australian stock saddle. Used for long periods at a time, this saddle has a longer weight bearing surface combined with a very comfortable seat. This pattern is used more and more for long distance riding.*

RIGHT: *Checking the girth. The rider has put her left arm through the reins so that she has some control over the horse without upsetting him with too tight a hold. This girth is too loose.*

BELOW RIGHT: *Checking that the stirrup leathers are approximately the correct length. This is a rough guide only but it does at least give you a chance to mount up without disaster. If you let the stirrups down too much to make this stage easier, you may find you can't reach the saddle to sit down without a struggle.*

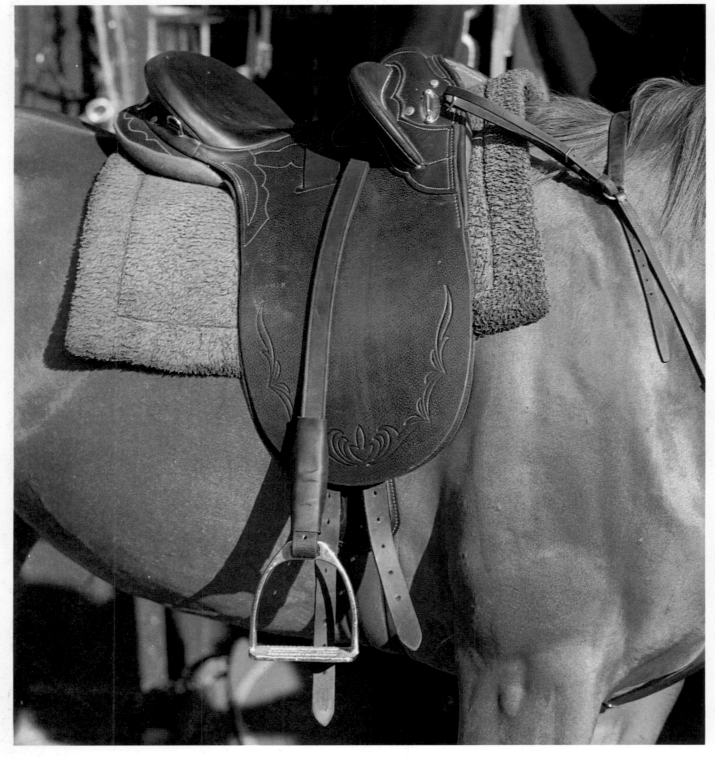

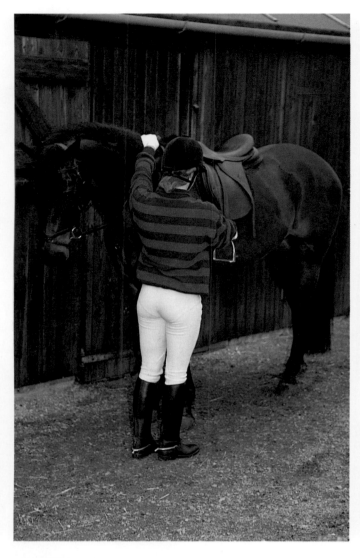
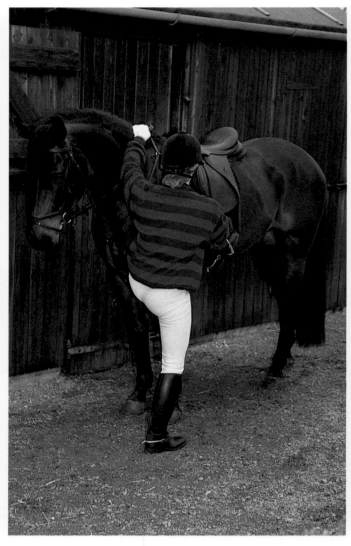

MOUNTING AND DISMOUNTING

Mounting is straightforward enough in theory, but a little more difficult in practise the first few times. Take the reins in your left hand so both are short enough to keep the horse under control yet not so tight that he goes into reverse. It is quite acceptable to hold a piece of mane in your left hand as well. It will not hurt the horse should you tug it slightly, and is preferable to pulling on the reins and therefore his mouth. Steady the stirrup with the other hand while you put your left foot firmly into it. Pushing your toe down will aid your balance and avoid digging the horse in the ribs. Then put your right hand anywhere on the front half of the saddle. If you hold the back of the saddle, the saddle may twist and you'll find that you have nowhere to sit when you get up there as your arm will be in the way. Bouncing a couple of times on your right foot before you go for the big one will give you some height and spring. Go up as quickly and lightly as you can, swinging your right leg clear of the horse's rump.

Sit down softly for the horse's sake and you're there. It can be an odd feeling at first, sitting high on a living animal. Try to sit up while you find your other stirrup — it's a feeling you will quickly get used to. Whether you ride English or Western style, the balance and basic position are the same. Sit up as tall as you can, shoulders wide, head up, back straight. Just as if you were standing on the ground, keep a straight line running down from your shoulder, through your hip to your heel. It is not easy to judge how you look without a mirror, so if you can, avoid either forcing your legs back or forwards, and you won't be too far wrong. Sit it the lowest part of the saddle — most beginners tend to sit too far back. Only tighten the muscles you really need, so your legs can be relaxed, your seat muscles softened and your back, shoulders and neck only braced enough to prevent you from slumping.

If you need to alter the length of your stirrups, this can be done one-handed, so that the other hand is free to hold the reins and control the horse. With both feet free of the stirrups and your legs hanging without tension, the bottom of the stirrup iron should be approximately level with the ankle bone. This is a comfortable length for most people and after a few rides it will not be necessary to take your feet out of the stirrups to check. If it feels right, it probably is right. Adjust the leathers, with your feet remaining in the stirrups by holding the spare leather in your hand and using your index finger to control the tongue of the buckle. Either pull the spare end up to shorten your stirrups or let it through as you

ABOVE, LEFT TO RIGHT: *Following this system means that getting on a horse is safe and simple. Take careful note of each stage so that you are clear in your mind of what you do. When faced for the first time, with a rather knowing and off-putting horse, it is easy to become confused.*

By keeping hold of the reins, the horse is never left out of control. Some horses will take a few steps forward, but this will not matter if you start by facing the tail.

RIGHT: *This rider looks comfortable and is in control of her horse.*

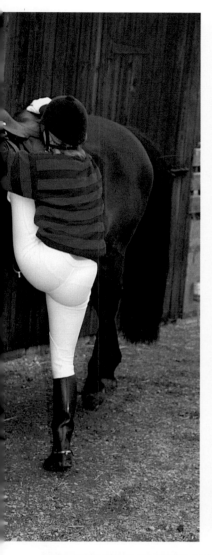

push down on the iron with your foot to lengthen the stirrup. This is a knack which requires practice. It is easier to use two hands but much less safe, as it means you have no control over the horse while you are getting settled in.

When you are ready, hold one rein in each hand. From the horse's head, the reins should run up through the hand towards the thumb, the spare end falling over your index finger. Light pressure from your thumb will stop them slipping through your hand. Hold your reins firmly but gently. Too strong a grip will be tiring, make your hands sore and upset the horse. Slack hands will mean losing the reins. Keep your reins of equal length so the horse's head is straight and he can move in a straight line when you start walking. Keep your elbows bent and close to your sides.

To dismount, put both reins into your left hand, leaving your right hand free to hold the front of saddle. Take both feet out of the irons. In one movement, ease your weight out of the saddle and swing your right leg up and over the horse's back. Land lightly on both feet, letting your knees bend to avoid jarring.

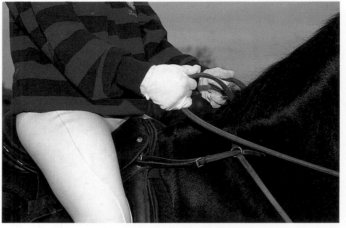

LEFT: *Holding the reins incorrectly. This methods provides a weak grip and the horse's mouth will be insensitive to it.*

BELOW LEFT: *The correct method of holding the reins. The rein should run from the bit (horse's mouth) to the lower part of the hand and up through the palm. A steady hold is maintained with light thumb pressure on the spare end of the reins. Notice also that the rider's hands are carried and are not resting on the horse's neck. This makes it easier to give clear aids (commands) to the horse.*

ABOVE: *Preparing to dismount, both feet free of the irons, reins still in contact so that control over the horse is not lost. It is important not to leave the left foot in the iron.*

RIGHT: *Swing your leg well clear of the horse's rump – keeping your leg almost straight makes it easier to get a good swing and avoids getting caught on the back of the saddle.*

BELOW: *Down safely and still next to the horse and in control. The rein on the off is is now slack so the rider has not pulled the horse's mouth on landing.*

RIGHT: *A safe and balanced general purpose position in the saddle. A straight line could be drawn through the rider's shoulder, hip and down to the heel. Her feet might be a little further into the irons for a better grip. However, this rider looks neat, elegant and confident.*

MOVING OFF

In order to control a horse, a rider relies on a set of commands or 'aids'; these are widely-used actions that make a horse behave as the rider wishes. They are divided into natural aids – the hands, legs and seat – and artificial aids such as spurs or whips.

Your legs will make the horse go forwards and your hands will stop him or slow him down. To get him to walk forwards, close your lower legs against his sides and squeeze. Sit up tall while you do this, keeping your legs pushed down. It is a great temptation to grip up but this will result in losing your stirrups. Should the horse take no notice, repeat the command (aid) as often as necessary, using your legs more strongly each time. Kicking with the back of the heel is a common sight but can lead to disastrous results on a willing horse – he will go forward much faster than you intended! A lazy horse used to beginners may expect and want to be 'kicked' forwards, but repeated kicking deadens the sides and makes him gradually more difficult to ride.

To stop again, apply light pressure on his mouth equally with both hands bringing your shoulders back at the same time. A well-trained horse will respond if you just close your fingers on the reins, like squeezing water out of a sponge. It is a good idea to practice stopping and starting a few times before trying anything more ambitious while you get used to the feel of the horse. They are all different and you can quickly

get the feel of how strong your aids need to be for individual animals. It will give you great confidence to know that you can stop if you need to.

It is worth mentioning here that horses accustomed to beginners do not always seem very responsive. In a way, this is a good thing, because if you lose your balance and either pull him in the mouth or dig his sides with your heels by accident, he isn't going to shoot off in a panic. It is like learning a foreign language — at first, what you are trying to tell the horse may not always be clear to him, and he may misunderstand. Do not be impatient with the horse if this is the case. As you gain experience, you'll find the horse responding better and more immediately.

Steering requires the use of both legs and hands. To turn the horse to the left, gently pull on your left rein to bring his head round to the left. Increase the use of your right leg to bring his body round into the turn. Whenever you use the reins, you will find it necessary to use both legs to some extent to keep the horse going forwards, maintaining his rate of progress. Turn your body slightly to the left and look left yourself. Turning right, therefore, will mean using more left leg with your right rein. Practice a few turns so that you and the horse can gain confidence in each other. With both slowing down and turning, only apply the aid until the horse starts to respond. Once he has started to move as the rider wishes,

his good behavior can be rewarded by letting him carry on without any interference from the rider.

A horse's walk creates a lot of movement in his back. You may feel that you are rolling from side to side. If you remain sitting tall with your head and shoulders as steady as possible, you will be able to absorb this movement in your hips and pelvis. The more tense you are, the harder this will be, so keep telling yourself to relax the muscles in your seat and lower back. Both you and the horse will be more comfortable when you do this, and you will find the work less tiring. In order to become accustomed to controlling the horse, to learn how to sit properly, and to tone your 'riding muscles', it is best just to keep walking at first. Trotting and cantering are much bouncier gaits, requiring far more stability and providing less 'thinking time', so make the most of walking while you can. Experienced riders always return to working in walk to sort out any problems either with their own riding or the horse's way of going. It is a habit worth copying.

FAR LEFT: *Just like their riders, horses enjoy each others company. These two riders are sitting well and are dressed safely (note hats with chinstraps) and practically for hacking out.*

ABOVE LEFT: *A good seat is easier to establish in walk and is a pleasant way to enjoy a summer's day. Riding with a friend will help you relax and feel natural on a horse.*

LEFT: *The trot feels much faster at first. This experienced rider makes it look easy.*

ABOVE: *Under instruction with the Pony Club.*

RIGHT: *This rider is in competition. Her tension can be seen in her jutting chin, straight arms and lower legs held away from her pony's side because her knees have locked. These faults are easy enough to correct once the rider is aware of the problem.*

Equine Movement

The horse has four basic gaits – walk, trot, canter, and gallop. Each has its own rhythm and feels distinctly different to ride. Knowing how the horse is moving underneath you may not seem relevant at first, but it will become more and more important as your riding improves.

When walking, each of the horse's legs moves in turn, no two legs moving together. At no time does the horse have all four legs off the ground at once. From halt he can move any leg first, but if starting with a hind leg, the foreleg on the same side is next to move. The sequence, therefore, is off hind, off fore, near hind, off fore. This explains the side-to-side rolling motion felt from the saddle.

The trot is a two-time gait, the horse now pairing his legs by springing from one diagonal pair to the other. Between each diagonal pair striking the ground there is a brief moment of complete suspension. Trotting is the bounciest gait to ride, and it is much more difficult for the beginner to balance and maintain position. This is why the 'rising trot' emerged; the rider stands up and sits down to follow the movement of one diagonal pair of legs, rising as one pair leaves the ground, and sitting as the same pair returns. Trotting is more comfortable and less tiring once the rising trot has been mastered.

The canter is a three-time gait. The horse progresses forward in a series of steady bounds with a moment of suspension between each bound. From the moment of suspension, the footfall order is: one hind leg, a diagonal pair, finally the remaining foreleg. To balance himself safely in turns, the horse should finish the sequence with his inside foreleg, known as the 'leading' leg. In canter left, the footfalls are – off hind, right diagonal pair (near hind and off fore together) and lastly the near fore.

Viewed from the ground, the leading leg actually appears to be in front, which is why it is called the 'leading leg'. A free horse will change the lead automatically when he changes direction in canter.

The gallop is, of course, the fastest of the four gaits. The horse now moves in four time, each leg moving separately. It differs in sequence from the walk, as the horse moves each hind leg in turn, followed by each front leg in turn. Starting from the moment of suspension, in a left turn, we now have off hind, near hind followed by off fore, rear fore.

Cantering is more comfortable than trotting and the gallop is the most comfortable of the faster gaits to ride – once you are used to the speed. Galloping, however, is not recommended for beginners as the process of slowing down through the gaits can be rather unseating.

44

The walk with the near fore about to leave the ground, and near hind ready to come forward. The horse's weight is taken on both off side legs. The roll of the walk can be felt as the weight transfers to the near side legs and vice versa.

OPPOSITE PAGE, BELOW: *Walking, showing four clear beats as no two legs are paired.*

THIS PAGE, ABOVE LEFT: *The walk. Weight now borne on near-side legs.*

ABOVE: *Trotting. Weight now carried on a diagonal pair of legs. The 'right' diagonal is off the ground.*

THIS PAGE, FAR LEFT: *Trotting – left diagonal is lifting.*

LEFT: *Walking. The off fore wil lift to allow the off hind to come forward.*

ABOVE LEFT: *Sitting to the trot. With the reins in one hand, you can hold the front of the saddle with the other, without using the reins for balance.*

ABOVE: *This rider has tightened her seat muscles and is tipping forward slightly. She is, however, able to sit very still in trot because she has a secure hold on the saddle.*

LEFT: *Sitting trot without holding on. The rider is using a certain amount of leg grip to steady her seat but is still able to keep still and not interfere with the horse's mouth. If she leant back slightly more she could lose some of the tension in her leg muscles.*

TROTTING

The first trot will feel fast and bumpy. It is desirable to hold on to the neckstrap if your horse is wearing one, or the front arch of the saddle, while you get the feel of this new movement. Maintain your position in the saddle as for walk. Sit up straight, push your legs down with your weight going into the heel and keep your seat down in the saddle. It is natural to be tense at first, but try to allow the movement from the horse to be absorbed into your back and seat. This requires some suppleness, but will ensure that you feel more comfortable.

To start the trot, use your legs just as you did to go from halt to walk — both together. Keep them close to the horse's sides once you are trotting but only squeeze enough to keep him going. If you grip with the lower leg for balance the horse may think you want to go faster. To return to walk use the same aid as for walk to halt. Use both reins evenly for just long enough to slow down and not stop completely. If you are still holding on for balance, then simply not using your legs will allow the horse to slow down.

The rising trot is not used in Western riding. Western saddles are designed for extreme comfort over long distances without jumping, so that sitting to the trot is really quite comfortable. With a general purpose saddle used in English style, which includes jumping, the rising trot is essential until you are quite advanced.

RIGHT: *Full Western turnout. The rider sits tall and comfortably in the saddle with long stirrups. This position is maintained through all the gaits and is made easy through the design of the saddle. Likewise, the pressure on the horse's mouth through the reins remains light. Western-style bits are more severe than English unless correctly handled, as in this photograph. Emulating this posture in the saddle is good for either method of riding.*

Step one is to feel the rhythm of the trot, while holding on to anything but the reins for balance. This is simple: say to yourself while trotting, bump – bump – bump – bump, then change the wording tn one – two – one – two.

Step two is to lift your weight on beat one and sit down for beat two. A demonstration at this point is a great help to show what you are aiming for. Practice the technique of shifting your weight in walk. In trot, the horse's movement will do most of the work for you. Avoid trying to stand too high each time but rather stay very close to the saddle. This prevents a double bounce as you sit down which makes it difficult to follow the rhythm. Having become used to the rising trot, you can comfortably let go of the saddle knowing you will not fall back on the reins and pull the horse in the mouth.

These pictures show the rising trot. The rider is taking care not to rise too high and so lose balance.

RIGHT: *The closer one can stay to the saddle while rising to the trot, the better.*

As explained earlier rising to the trot means moving in time with one diagonal pair of legs. It is important to change diagonal quite frequently to avoid the horse becoming one-sided. Before trying to change diagonal, first work out which diagonal you are riding on. The left diagonal refers to the left fore and the right hind. If this pair is on the ground as you sit, it is known as 'sitting on the left diagonal'. By watching the horse's shoulders in walk, you will see them moving back and forth, back when the foot is on the ground. Watch for this movement in trot. Whichever shoulder is coming back as you sit will indicate which diagonal you are sitting on.

To change diagonal, the rider does a double bump by sitting for two steps then continuing on the other diagonal. Glance down at the shoulders to check that you were successful and then look up again to see where you're going. Go over this change again as often as you need until you are sure you can change diagonal without looking down.

It is better for the horse's balance to sit on the outside diagonal through turns. He naturally carries three-fifths of his weight on the forelegs, so this method lessens the likelihood of straining his inside foreleg. Make frequent checks on your diagonals until you instinctively use the outside diagonal all the time. Remember to change diagonals from time to time when you ride out to balance the horse's workload.

The aid for turning remains the same as in walk. It is important to remember to use your legs to keep the horse trotting, in particular, the inside leg. The outside leg is still directing the turn but it is the inside leg which maintains impulsion. To avoid confusion, keep your inside leg in the normal position (known as 'on the girth') or slightly forward, while the outside leg is used slightly further back (behind the girth). Downward pressure on your inside heel is helpful as this shifts your weight in the direction of the turn. The horse will always tend to go in the direction your weight takes him.

These three pictures are all of the rising trot. Whichever diagonal pair of legs is off the ground while the rider is out of the saddle, shows you which diagonal the rider is riding on or sitting on.

BELOW: *Left diagonal. The rider will sit when the left diagonal returns to the ground.*

RIGHT: *Right diagonal.*

BELOW RIGHT: *Left diagonal.*

CANTERING

Cantering should wait until you are competent in trot. To get a canter, have your horse in an active trot, preferably on a circle or coming into a turn. Sit to the trot. Use your inside leg on the girth (for impulsion) and your outside leg behind the girth to get the strike off into canter. Keep an even contact on the reins taking care not to draw back on the inside rein. Sit up tall, shoulders back, seat well down in the saddle.

Again, it is advisable to hold on to the saddle or neckstrap while you get used to the rhythm. As you feel each step of canter, try to sit deep in the saddle and send your hips forward. Cantering provides a more rocking motion than the trot and is actually more comfortable. As you approach a turn, push your inside leg down, as in the trot, so that you can stay with the horse. This helps to prevent falling on the first corner if you have got out of rhythm and are unable to keep your seat in the saddle.

Until you are supple enough to follow easily the canter movement, it helps to count out each stride to yourself — down-two-three, down-two-three. Each time you say 'down', push your seat down and your heels down. Look up and ahead, staying in the saddle.

As explained earlier, the inside foreleg should be the leading leg through a turn. By shifting your outside leg back in asking for canter, you are directing the horse to make the correct sequence for a correct lead. A glance down at the horse's shoulders once you are in canter will tell you which leg is leading. The shoulder on that side will be further forward than the other. As soon as possible, try to judge which leg is leading by feel and not by looking down, which jeopardizes your balance.

Getting the correct lead in canter is essential if you are going to ride through a turn. If he is on the wrong leg, the horse will be forced to break gait (trot), lose the correct sequence of canter ('go disunited') or risk falling. A well schooled horse will be able to turn with an outside lead, if he is correctly ridden, or will make a neat 'flying change of lead'. If you have a wrong 'strike off', return to trot and try again.

These pictures show different stages of the canter left. In all, it is possible to pick out the right diagonal (off fore and near hind together). Also, the rider can clearly be seen sitting down in the saddle whilst still allowing some slight movement of the upper body in accordance with the canter strides.

The near fore is the leading leg (see top left), here clearly taking a big forward stride. Compare this with bottom left, opposite page. Notice the rider's legs staying on the horse's side, near the girth.

Technical Improvement

here are three basic ways to improve your riding. One is by riding out with a more experienced rider who can offer advice and encouragement. Another is to have group lessons, when it is up to you to work on your weaknesses and strengths while others have the instructor's attention. A third method is to have private lessons which will include work on the lunge. There are advantages and disadvantages in each.

With the instructor's individual attention, there is little chance that bad habits will develop. You can learn at your own speed, and progress should be quite fast. These lessons are necessarily shorter than class lessons so could leave you lacking actual time on the horse. If you feel you have a problem to overcome, this is probably the best way to do it.

During lunge lessons the horse is worked on a circle by the instructor. A lunge rein is attached to a lunge cavesson which is fitted over the bridle. Side reins running from the bit to the girth make sure the horse is well under control and works correctly. By these means, the rider is free to work on his balance and position without worrying about where or how the horse goes. All riders, of whatever standard, can benefit enormously from a course of lunge lessons. Exercises which will help balance, suppleness and confidence can often only be done by this method of teaching, so it is well worth booking a few lunge lessons to boost your riding ability. One word of warning – these lessons are much harder work than they look. Twenty minutes on the lunge is equivalent to about an hour and a half riding out in terms of effort.

LEFT: *Hacking out with a friend is a good opportunity to practise what you have been taught and enjoy your riding without feeling self-conscious.*

ABOVE: *If you are anxious about riding out due to your inexperience, accompanying more experienced riders should give you self-confidence. Here, a novice is sandwiched between two capable riders, who can ensure that she cannot get into difficulties. The same method is used when taking green horses out for the first time.*

RIGHT: *A horse correctly equipped for a lunge lesson. Notice the side-reins, the lunge cavesson to which the lunge rein attaches, and the protective boots on the horse's legs. This saddle is particularly appropriate as it will encourage the rider to sit correctly with minimum effort.*

There are several exercises which can be done not only during a lunge lesson, but also on the ground in your own time. Good posture in the saddle is essential for safe and effective riding but is very hard to achieve if the rest of your time is spent slouching or moving about badly. A typical example is a rounded back with shoulders drooping forwards and the head down. People who spend a lot of time working at a desk frequently have this problem, as do mothers with small children. Any occupation which takes the attention below eye level brings about the same result and it will require a great deal of effort to bring the body into a taller, more open outlook. Good posture has many long-term benefits, aside from riding horses – it can relieve tension, lessen the likelihood of back problems, aching shoulders, shortness of breath – the list is endless. The end result, therefore, is well worth the effort.

In riding, the seat is the most important part of the anatomy. Being able to soften the seat muscles in order to absorb all that activity from the horse without bouncing around, means being well balanced in the upper part of the body. The head is the single, heaviest part of the human body in relation to its size, so it is logical to start at the top and work down.

RIGHT: *This shows a good basic position, although the rider's lower leg is slightly too far back. With no worries about getting the horse moving the rider can quickly get the feel of holding the position as the horse goes through the gaits.*

FAR RIGHT: *Circling arms backwards in walk. This rider is sufficiently confident not to hold the saddle, although it is quite acceptable to do this at first.*

FAR RIGHT BELOW: *Shoulder shrugging leaving the hands in normal position.*

BELOW: *On the lunge in trot. The reins are knotted but within reach so the rider is able to hold the saddle while working on her position.*

ABOVE: *How a day's work can wind you up! Tense shoulders, neck and head usually need most attention with a part-time rider.*

PREVIOUS PAGE: *The rider will find it easier to do exercises without a jacket, a sweater allowing greater freedom of movement. This should not be so enormous as to hide the rider's movements from the instructor.*

EXERCISES

Head and neck exercises can be done anywhere at any time. Imagine somebody is pulling you up by your ears and stretching your neck to its fullest length. As you do this, you should immediately feel that you are expanding and widening your chest. Look around, use your eyes and then turn your head in either direction. This way, you will not stiffen and look like a soldier on parade. Try to keep this lengthened neck all the time, particularly when you are doing other exercises. Do it when you take a break from poring over a desk, or washing up, digging the garden or whatever you feel draws your head down and your chin into your chest, and whenever you are walking or running about.

To relieve stiffness, roll your head round, bringing each ear in turn towards your shoulder, pushing your head back as far as possible and forwards to stretch the back of your neck. Finish with a backward roll before bringing your head once again to the tall position. This is another exercise that can be done anywhere and leads neatly into the first shoulder exercise.

SHOULDERS AND ARMS

Pull your shoulders up towards your ears and then push them down again as far as possible, in a shrugging movement. With arms straight down by your sides, make a fist with each hand in turn, which will help the downward push. Shoulders are particularly vulnerable to tension as a result of stress. One of the classic symptoms of stress are hunched shoulders combined with the head thrusting forwards. If you suffer from this, you may not be aware of it until you try to use your shoulder muscles. Then you discover just how much a hectic day has tightened you up. By positively using these tight muscles, you will be much better able to relax them. The relief is almost exhilarating. Continue this process by rolling each shoulder in turn and then both together — forwards, up, back and down. Leave your arms hanging by your sides.

The next exercise includes your arms and does require a bit of space. The earlier exercises can be performed even on a crowded train, but not this one. Taking each arm in turn, raise your hand to shoulder height, stretched as far out in front as you can reach. Very slowly, raise your arm above your head and continue round behind to make a complete circle, always with your arm straight and fingers extended, but not rigid. Reach as far as you can all the way round. If you are right handed you may find this easier with your right arm and vice versa if you are left-

handed. It is important to become as ambidextrous as possible so that each side of your body works equally well when you are riding.

It is worthwhile assessing how ambidextrous you are in your day-to-day life. For example, if you carry a shoulder bag over the same shoulder all the time, that shoulder will be higher and more developed than the other. If you play a racket sport you will probably have to work quite hard at rebalancing your body. See if you can circle your arms in opposite directions simultaneously, with each in turn taking the backward circle as described. This is good for coordination, and it will demonstrate just how even-sided you are.

A third shoulder and arm exercise which is good for overall posture is to stand (or ride on the lunge) with both arms held out sideways at shoulder height, fingers extended. Have both hands slightly above and behind your shoulders. This willl strengthen your upper arms and shoulders, although it is also very tiring.

BACK, WAIST AND CHEST

Arm and shoulder exercises will have improved the position of your upper body already, so the following exercises are really a continuation, and still involve arm movement. All can be achieved on horseback, and will help beginners with their stability. The natural contours of the spine are often lost through tension and resulting poor posture, particularly the gentle forward curve of

the small of the back. In the early days of riding you may find yourself wanting to crouch low to sit as close to the horse as possible, which will make your back round and stiff. This restricts movement of the chest wall and will lead to shallow breathing.

With these simple exercises, the aim is to stretch the body, lengthen the waist, realign the backbone and expand the chest. They will also help to build up your confidence as your balance on horseback improves.

STRETCHING

Bring your arms up to shoulder height, stretched forwards. Slowly raise them above your head as if stretching up to reach something above you. You

Keeping your hands level in this exercise (top right) and your arms in line with the radius of the circle, will encourage straightness as well as the other benefits mentioned in the text.

ABOVE LEFT: *Arm*

can still look where you are going while you allow your whole body to lengthen, especially through the waist. Hold this for as long as you feel comfortable and then slowly lower your arms and hands to normal riding position. Keep the length in your waist and don't shrink back to a hunched position.

ARM FOLDING

This is another exercise which is equally beneficial on or off the horse. Folding your arms across your chest rounds the shoulders, so try folding them behind your back. Get hold of both elbows with both hands and press your forearms into the small of your back. Don't attempt this on a horse unless you have somebody else in absolute control of the horse's movement. A few minutes of this exercise will really stretch and strengthen your abdominal muscles and back.

All these exercises can be done with or without stirrups. If you feel confident enough to go without, then cross your stirrups over in front of the saddle so that they don't swing around and bang into the horse's sides. Get the feel of each exercise in halt or walk and only attempt them at trot when you are really confident. Start with the easier exercises first so that you are able to hold on to the front of the saddle for balance. Trotting without stirrups and free hands is not easy, and a step or two at first is more than enough. Avoid strain by not overdoing any exercise.

stretching. This exercise will give your confidence a boost as it improves balance as well as posture. When you feel at ease with your arms above your head, you will feel less inclined to hold on to the saddle or reins for safety. This, in turn, will help your control over the horse.

TOP ROW: *Three stages of circling arms backwards. Keeping your head still ensures maximum benefit in the movement of the shoulder joints without loss of balance. It will also strengthen the weaker side and will improve the equal usage of left and right sides.*

ABOVE: *This rider is demonstrating a very correct position while probably concentrating on her arms. A good riding position is natural and should feel comfortable.*

SEAT AND LEGS

Throughout all your work, keep you seat muscles as soft as possible, so that your hips can follow the swing of the horse's back. Clenching these muscles is instinctive and it is only through constantly reminding yourself that you will overcome this difficulty. To get the idea of just how much movement you should take from the horse, through your hips and pelvis, try walking (off the horse) with a book on your head. This creates exactly the same movement you should get in your pelvis when you are on the horse. Once back on the horse, aim to keep the same stillness in your head and shoulders, absorbing the movement with your lower body. Having got the hang of it, riding long distances at walk, which you would do on a riding holiday, becomes less tiring, and you will give the horse a much more comfortable ride too.

With your feet free of the stirrups, let your legs hang from the hips down the horse's sides. Any gripping is unnecessary unless the horse plays up and you need to avoid falling off. In this case, knee and thigh grip can be quite useful. The weight of your legs will be enough to pull them down without straining to ride 'long'. Tighten and release each group of muscles in turn – seat, thighs, calves – so that you immediately become aware of unnecessary tension. Keeping your knees against the saddle, slowly swing your lower legs back and forth, taking care not to kick the horse. As one leg goes forward, the other goes back. This exercise is helpful in giving controlled leg aids.

With each foot in turn, stretch your toes downwards, upwards and round in a circle. Supple ankles will work as springs and play an important role in shock absorbing as your riding becomes more ambitious. This is an exercise to

do under the desk at work, with each leg crossed over in turn. When riding, you will, of course, have to do this one without stirrups. Working your feet independently — for example, stretch the toes of one foot down while rotating the other — will help your coordination.

These exercises are basic and simple. There are many more to be tried, including some more ambitious gymnastic exercises. It is not the degree of difficulty which counts but the end result, so if you feel worse as a result of trying any particular exercise, don't do it. There is nothing to be gained from straining or frightening yourself — the aim is to improve your balance, control, suppleness and confidence. Whatever type of riding you undertake, all these points are important. With this in mind, as you improve, you will find that all horses are more than willing to do as you ask: the more confident the rider, the better the horse will feel.

TOP: *Stretching toes down. Care must be taken not to tighten the shoulder muscles when working on leg muscles. This rider's left shoulder has lifted and come forward.*

LEFT: *Lower leg swinging. In this relatively simple exercise, more attention can be given to keeping* the shoulders square to the horse's shoulders, the neck free and the spine in correct alignment, than in actually moving the legs.

ABOVE: *Lifting the legs clear of the saddle is a strenuous exercise which cannot be maintained for more* than very brief periods. It will certainly encourage you to sit down in the saddle and not perch! The value of this exercise is clear when it is over, when you will be more aware of your leg position.

Until you are fit you will doubtless have days when you are sore and aching after riding, particularly on the following day. The best way to cope with this is to keep moving as much as possible. A soak in a hot bath always helps to relax tired muscles. Wearing the right clothing will help prevent blisters from the saddle or stirrup leathers; avoid seams where you take most weight or friction, for example. Experience will soon tell you if you need a change of style.

If you are planning to go trekking, on a riding holiday or for an intensive course of lessons, get as much time in the saddle as possible before you go. It is a pity to ruin a holiday through being in too much pain to get out of bed in the morning, simply because you did not prepare sufficiently before leaving. Once your riding muscles are in trim, life on a horse becomes much more pleasant.

LEFT AND ABOVE: *Trotting without stirrups while someone else looks after your horse is a marvelous way to get used to the feel of the horse's movement. It will be some time before you can let go of the saddle without losing balance, at least without stirrups. Even an experienced rider (as here) gets more benefit from the lesson while holding on.*

TOP: *A good exercise for her – turning her head without losing her straightness. A few head rolls now would perfect a nice picture.*

RIGHT: *Time to relax and enjoy the benefit of all that hard work.*

Hacking and Jumping

If you are confident and in reasonable control of a quiet horse in the slower gaits, now is the time to think about progressing to something more ambitious – riding out, jumping, galloping, and perhaps trying a livelier horse. Nothing in riding is difficult if you know what to expect and have a general idea of how to adapt your basic riding technique. All horses are different, and you will never stop learning or improving as long as you keep an open mind and are prepared to have a go. Any time you feel genuinely frightened, though, hold back and wait until your confidence improves. Fear is transmitted to the horse and will affect his behavior. In addition, if you panic, you are far more likely to forget everything you have learned, and may make dangerous errors.

Knowing you can control your nerves is a different matter. Part of the thrill of riding is in the challenge of being able to achieve things of which you didn't know you were capable. This is where a good instructor is essential. Such a person will know whether or not your ability is up to a good gallop, a bigger jump, a particular horse, and will

be able to spur you on. There is no substitute for somebody with greater knowledge saying 'Yes, you can do it!' There is also a lot of truth in the saying that a little knowledge can be a dangerous thing, so avoid launching out on your own just yet and don't try to do things for which you have not been trained.

JUMPING

The jumping position is used not only for jumping but also for fast work and some hill work. The position can be learned and practiced in the slower gaits so that when you make your first gallop or jump, you will be pleasantly surprised at how easy it is, and you will have avoided unnecessary risks. Perhaps a better description of the jumping position is the 'forward-seat'. It was a technique developed mainly in Italy earlier this century, amid much controversy and ridicule. A glance at old hunting prints will show earlier riding styles which were thought to be fairly safe in their day. The problem was that by sitting up

ABOVE: *These riders are demonstrating what could be called the 'modern hunting seat'. Jumping natural fences holds a certain amount of mystery – could there be a ditch or a drop on the far side of a thick hedge? There is a tendency always to keep the lower leg further forward than is ideal for balance – just in case it turns out to be a long way down. Everyone accepts that to lean forward is essential to allow the horse to jump freely, hence this slightly awkward but effective hunting seat.*

ABOVE RIGHT: *This gentleman has got a bit left behind so that his center of gravity is so far back as to make the horse jump awkwardly. Note the uncomfortable bunching up of the horse's hindlegs. Even so, the rider is making a great effort to give with his hands and not to pull his horse's head back and up.*

RIGHT: *The hunting seat again – this time the rider has really let the horse stretch to produce a superb jump.*

with the weight down in the saddle, the horse was forced to jump with a hollow back and legs trailing. This is unnatural and probably brought about many more falls of both horse and rider than happen today. The argument against the forward seat was, that should the horse stop suddenly, the rider would shoot over his head. In fact, if the rider uses the forward seat properly, his balance is so good that it takes an awful lot to dislodge him at all. When you are learning this new seat, you should feel safe and secure. If not, it is because something is not right and you should try to find out what you are doing wrong before going any further.

In normal riding, the line of balance is shoulder, hip, heel — a straight line running through these points will be vertical. Starting with shorter stirrups, the forward seat transfers this line to shoulder, knee, ankle, with the shoulder being the most forward point. The weight is taken off the horse's back and transferred to the rider's knee and ankle/heel. The

rider looks ahead with his shoulders wide and his back flat — not rounded — and with knees and heels pushed well down.

Knee gripping is not normally used when riding on the flat, but is important for stability when jumping. To achieve a good grip turn the toes out very slightly so that the big toe joint has the strongest contact with the stirrup iron. With a good bend in the knees and ankles, 'folding' the upper body forward from the hip joint should be easy and relatively effortless. Allow your seat to move back as you fold your weight off the saddle and test your balance. If it is correct, your arms will be free to move as you wish and you will not need to hold on to anything for extra stability. By transferring your weight to your knees and heels so that you are supported either side of the horse rather than on top, you should be sitting in a secure position.

Elbows should be bent as normal, the hands remaining in position just above or near the base of the horse's neck. How far to shorten the stirrups will depend on the rider's height and suppleness, and will vary between one and seven holes. Usually two or three holes shorter is adequate for general riding.

A saddle with a forward cut is suitable for riding with shorter stirrups. The flap is cut forward from the line of the pommel to give support to the rider's knee and thigh. Knee rolls at the front of the saddle prevent the rider from slipping forward on to the horse's shoulders.

To check your balance and get a general idea of how the two styles of riding compare, try them out on foot, preferably in front of a mirror. Take the upright position first, standing sideways on

RIGHT: *An enthusiastic instructor giving a jumping lesson. The most important early lesson is to go forward and 'allow' with the hands. Using low cross poles such as this will help the horse jump smoothly and give the rider every chance to work on his technique. Ground poles are helpful in putting the horse on a good stride for the jump and also to help the rider get a straight approach.*

ABOVE: *This picture clearly shows how the ground pole has put the horse exactly right for take-off, leaving the rider more able to concentrate on herself. She is demonstrating a very strong lower leg position, making good use of her ankles to anchor her position. This in turn has secured her knees comfortably to the knee roll.*

LEFT: *This rider has actually gone too far up and forward, although in a moment, when the horse is further over the jump, she will look better. During the early stages of learning to jump, this is a fault in the right direction. It still leaves the horse free to jump safely and the rider will be able to modify her forward seat with experience.*

to the mirror. Stand up straight, with your weight spread evenly across from your big toe joints, to the outside edges of your feet and into your heels. Place your feet wide enough apart to allow room for a horse and then bend your knees without leaning forwards. Check for the line, shoulder-hip-heel. Leaving your elbows close to your sides, raise your hands to riding position. Now turn your toes slightly outwards so that you can take more weight on your big toe joints and heels with much less on the outside edge of your feet. Increase the bend in your knees as you lower your shoulders, so that your forearms come closer to your knees but stay parallel to the ground. This is the forward seat. As long as your back is flat and your knees bent, heel down, you cannot go far wrong without literally falling over. Holding this position for increasing periods will strengthen your leg and back muscles ready for the real thing. Educating your body to the right feel is a great help, too.

LEFT: *Practising without reins will certainly ensure that riders do not use them to balance!*

BELOW: *Learn to look around (for the jump) while riding strongly forward. A good jump comes from good flat work.*

POLE WORK

Jumping over fallen branches, small streams or whatever natural objects you meet while riding out, is the easiest way to learn to jump. If a group of horses all pop over quite happily, then the rest will follow without much say-so from the rider. If you are lucky enough to be able to ride a trained horse in this way, then all you need do is hold on, get into position and follow the herd. After two or three jumps you will probably feel bold enough to tackle anything − after all, a jump is only a big stride of canter. The trouble with natural obstacles can be size − a fallen tree across a forest path may be a bit too big for a first effort. Jumping is always worth working on in the school, so that you can be in charge and not the horse; in this situation the fences can be adjusted to suit each horse and rider's ability.

Starting with a single pole on the ground will give you an idea of riding straight towards the middle of the obstacle. Although you may not get even the slightest hop over the pole from the horse, ride with a degree of positiveness. Ideally, the horse maintains an active but steady rhythm in whichever gait is selected, trot or canter. Ride in forward seat. Keep up the momentum after the pole so that you keep the horse under orders. In

ABOVE LEFT: *This rider has a very strong and well-established forward seat. Her lower leg is staying securely in place, neither too far forward nor too far back. She has, however, pushed her hands much further forward than is necessary and so the reins are left flapping. This is not a difficult fault to correct.*

LEFT: *It is practical to have several people on a jumping lesson together as long as the horses have similar lengths of stride. This gives an opportunity for each horse and rider to rest, makes better use of the time and effort used to set up the poles and jumps, and the riders can learn from watching each other. A group jumping lesson invites mutual encouragement, which can speed progress.*

due course, you will probably want to jump more than one obstacle at a time, so this is a good habit to develop.

Place pairs of cones or markers about a meter and a half apart, on either side of the pole. If these are about 10m (30 feet) from the pole, they make a useful guide for riding straight before and after the jump. The pole can be approached from either direction, with a left or right turn, and the cones will give you an idea of the minimum distance you will need for a successful jump.

When the pole is raised to make a real jump, work in stages of about 5-10cm (3-5 inches) each time, while you get used to going 'with' the horse, getting the feel of when he is going to leave the ground. Some horses need driving on even to the smallest of jumps, while others need lots of calming circle work beforehand to stop them getting too fast. Generally, the less you interfere, the better. Do the minimum to keep him straight, forward-going and sensible, and let him do the jumping. This is enough for the first stage.

GALLOPING

The first gallop really gets the blood flowing through your veins. It is tremendously exciting, far easier than you may expect and (so long as you survive the slowing down process) something that you will want to do as often as possible. Remember though, that galloping is very taxing on any horse's physique, and should only be done on good going (ground that is neither too soft, nor rock hard), not too often, and very rarely at full speed.

Use the forward seat. Sandy beaches are ideal for galloping as there is room to build up speed gradually and room to slow down the same way. Grassy tracks, forest paths, open fields, are all good possibilities. Avoid galloping downhill – stopping and balancing are much more tricky. Push your horse forward to trot, then canter, making sure he is still paying attention to you and that you feel comfortable and secure. Then you can let him go – ease the contact on his mouth, push on with your legs and wait for the change of gear. It is not as marked a change as through the other gaits, rather a leveling off of the canter. You'll notice that the horse feels longer as he stretches and extends his head and neck to cover more ground. He does in fact become more difficult to steer until he slows again to canter. Keep your weight off his back and lean forward until you want to slow down.

As you sit back, the horse will check his speed. Use repeated slowing down aids as with the other gaits. If stopping is a problem, then pulling hard on both reins together will tire you

out and do nothing for the horse. When this happens, bring the horse into a turn, making the turn gradually tighter while your weight is pushed firmly into your inside leg. It is the outside rein which will do most to reduce the speed. Most horses will slow down of their own volition if you leave them alone and will certainly slow down with the others in a group.

The slowing down process will produce the bumpiest ride. As long as you sit back, keeping your legs underneath you – not stuck forwards or back – then there is no problem. 'Bridging' the reins can be helpful. This means holding the spare end of the reins in the opposite hands so that you have something to lean against over the horse's neck. You would really have to work hard at falling forwards if you do this.

ABOVE: *A brisk canter is less tiring than galloping at full speed.*

ABOVE RIGHT: *A perfect training ground for racehorses – good going and plenty of space.*

BELOW RIGHT: *Riding this short is only necessary for racing and is both difficult and dangerous for the amateur rider.*

OVERLEAF: *Lucinda Green. The perfect galloping seat.*

76

MISBEHAVIOR

No horse is a paragon of virtue all the time. Horses in general are notorious for being unpredictable, though it is fair to say that the older a horse gets, the more predictable is his behavior. Young horses by nature are playful and skittish until they get used to a bit of hard work, so it is well to be prepared for the more common misdemeanors.

Horses shy at the most ridiculous things. Plastic bags, umbrellas, holes in the ground, damp patches where the ground changes color, birds and anything which catches the light or moves unexpectedly. The more time you spend on their backs, the more you start to see things with an equine eye and can therefore be prepared.

Stopping to let a horse have a good long look at a 'spook' is often the safest remedy, just so long as he doesn't try to turn or run away. A lead from a more experienced horse will give a youngster the confidence he needs to go on and is better than bullying from the rider. Getting off to lead him past the object of his fear may work. You still have to get on again and if he is really frightened, you may have a problem holding on to him.

As long as whatever seems so horrifying isn't too serious, the best thing is to ride forward and straight. If the spook is coming up on the left, keep your right leg firm on his side, keep a good feel on the right rein so that he can't turn to face the problem. Shying at a paper bag on the roadside can leave a horse flying into oncoming traffic if he is allowed to turn and look, so this is important. Once you have passed his spook, always pat him to show that you're pleased he has pulled himself together.

Shying is often sudden and can leave you sitting on the ground wondering where on earth the horse has gone. Don't worry – as long as you are unhurt, climb straight back on again. The horse is not bad – you'll just have to keep a sharper look-out on his behalf and be more prepared next time.

BUCKING AND REARING

A lively horse can be expected to buck occasionally. It is more often a sign of exuberance than bad temper and it is very rare for a horse deliberately to throw a rider. Once a horse has learned to do this, an experienced rider with strong nerves should try to correct the problem. Bucking is most likely to occur on cold mornings if the horse

BELOW LEFT: *A refusal is not usually completely sudden and unexpected, and a resulting fall is hardly ever serious.*

BELOW: *Rearing is dangerous. This child rider has managed to lean forward in time and looks safe for the moment. She needs to get the pony going forward so this does not recur.*

FAR RIGHT, ABOVE AND BELOW: *The bucking and rearing demonstrated by this horse are termed 'napping'. The road is a bad place to have an argument because it is easy for a shod horse to slip and lose his footing. The rider here is keeping a cool head – no waving arms, reins or whips, so is giving herself a good chance to ride through this awkward moment.*

is short of exercise. Once he has warmed up and settled down, bucking should be over. If he continues to produce small bucks regardless of what work he has done, then he is probably suffering from backache or some other discomfort and will need checking over.

If you can jump a small fence and ride at speed, bucking is no problem and can in fact, be quite good fun (in small doses). Sit back, with long legs and seat down in the saddle. If there's time, grab a piece of mane, the neckstrap or the front of the saddle and sit tight. Keep your weight to the inside of any turns the horse chooses to make and your chances of coming off are slim.

Rearing, on the other hand, is nasty. A confirmed rearer should never be used on lessons or for novices. A horse standing up on his hind legs is precariously balanced and can all too easily fall backwards with the rider underneath. Nappy horses (horses who won't take the lead) will often do this if they are forced to go first or alone. A horse frightened by a severe bit or hamfisted rider may rear, too. If you find yourself sitting on a horse that starts to rear, then throw your arms round his neck so that you don't pull him over backwards. Tuck him in behind another horse and ride with as light a feel on the reins as possible to avoid a repetition.

FALLING OFF

It is difficult to avoid falling off for ever, however many precautions you take. If you know how to fall then there is no need to get hurt – unless you are very unlucky. Learning to fall in a gym is a great idea, especially for children. In the meantime, if you have time to think about it –

DON'T

* Put your hands out to save yourself, as you are more likely to break your wrists or collarbones.
* Try to hang on if the horse is clearly frightened, going faster and faster or trying to run away from you through fear. You'll only land harder and further from home.

DO

* Tuck your head in so that you can roll over in a somersault.
* Bring one arm across your chest to allow your shoulder lead into the roll.
* Always wear safe headgear.
* Try to relax; your body will absorb the impact more effectively.
* Hang on as long as possible if the horse is slowing down.
* Get straight back on unless you have really hurt yourself. The longer you leave it, the harder it will be to get your confidence back.

LEFT: *No chance of rolling here, but the rider is still in a good position with his chin towards his chest.*

BELOW: *A good roll in the making. This looks spectacular but it is unlikely that the rider would have been seriously hurt.*

RIGHT: *At this point the rider has no chance of recovery and can only think about making the fall as gentle as possible. If he looked up and lifted his chin, he could have been in very serious trouble.*

BELOW RIGHT: *As it was, he allowed himself to go with the fall and was therefore able to roll clear of the horse. Notice how his arms have instinctively come across his chest. In this picture he is flattening out again having rolled into a ball.*

Advanced Jumping and Cross Country

ross country riding involves tackling all sorts of obstacles, not necessarily to do with jumping. Most escorted hacks, treks or riding holidays cater for almost complete novices, and helpful advice may be given on the way. Being prepared, at least in theory if not in practice will, however, give the novice rider a much more confident start. A lot of trust may be put in horses or ponies accustomed to this sort of work. As with the first stages of jumping, the less interference they get, the better. The rider's main concern is to be sufficiently well-balanced to let the horse get on with his job.

WATER, HILLS AND NARROW PATHS

Riding through water is more a case of keeping dry than anything else. If a safe route across a flowing stream or river is not obvious, then tuck in behind the escort. Don't try to overtake or dictate which route should be taken or you may literally end up in deep water. Water drags on the horse's legs and will alter his gait accordingly — he will take slower, higher, bouncier steps. Rushing is more likely to cause him to lose his footing, so take your time. There is no harm in holding your feet up out of the water, just as long as this does not leave you hanging on the reins for balance. If you need extra support, hold the saddle or the mane.

Getting into and out of a stream or river is likely to necessitate going down and up some kind of a bank. Lean back on the way down to avoid pitching in head first. Keep the horse steady so that the water doesn't grab his legs as he goes in. Coming up the far bank is just the opposite. Lean forward and slacken the reins so that you don't get left behind as he bounds out. The mane makes a better handhold than the saddle should you need the support. The front of the

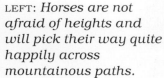

LEFT: *Horses are not afraid of heights and will pick their way quite happily across mountainous paths.*

ABOVE: *Sit quietly with loose reins and allow your horse to enjoy a good splash as he finds his way through deep water. Even if he does make a mistake and needs to swim, he will cope if he is allowed the freedom to do so.*

ABOVE RIGHT: *These competition horses out on exercise will benefit from walking through water. Apart from being cleansing, water is toning and refreshing so helps to keep the limbs in good order for more strenuous work. This picture shows clearly the exaggerated action made when going through water.*

RIGHT: *These long-distance competitors are allowing their horses to find their own footing across a rocky stream-bed. Going faster than a walk could cause injury to limbs and feet — even horse's hard hooves are prone to bruising.*

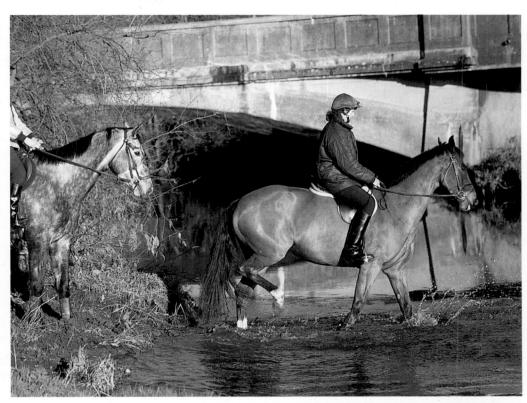

saddle is too close to you to be of much real help.

Riding up and down hills is a slightly different matter. On a long climb, the horse needs to get into a steady rhythm to preserve his energy and keep his breathing regular. If he rushes, he will lose momentum and have to stop for a rest. This is nerveracking as well as tiring. Sitting in the saddle without a change of basic position gives the best control and the easiest load to carry. If the hill is too steep to make a straight climb, then a series of traverses or zig zags is called for, otherwise a straight line up is the most sensible. Walking is the only gait suitable for a long climb.

Coming downhill is the same in reverse. Sit down in the saddle so that your upper body is vertical, not at right angles to the ground. Be quite sure that you are sitting straight in the saddle and that you allow yourself to absorb the increased movement from the horse's back. Rolling

from side to side is unhelpful, so you need the technique you worked on earlier, metaphorically riding with a book on your head. Aim for a steady rhythm, definitely no rushing but otherwise allow the horse to find his own footing.

The first time you tackle a narrow footpath traversing a mountainside, with a drop below you to one side and a sheer wall rising on the other, can be quite scary. Horses do not seem to have a fear of heights and will usually, with great calmness, pick their way along quite happily. It is a great temptation to lean to the side and look for the best footing, but this will of course, interfere. Horses can see very well and have no intention of making a mistake and falling. The only time he won't be able to see where he is going is if he is too close to the horse in front so that he is bumping into it. The best spacing is about one horse's length behind, close enough for the horse to feel secure, yet distant enough to look after himself.

BELOW LEFT: *Taken at the final of the Golden Horseshoe Ride on Exmoor, this picture shows three very fit and tough little horses, well used to coping with poor going underfoot. You will see again and again the experienced riders always make every effort to leave their horses free to sort themselves out and find their own balance with the lightest possible rein contact. A long-distance or cross-country horse becomes a real companion and not just a beast of burden, so mutual trust between horse and rider is very important.*

BELOW: *What better way to travel? Very few horses will bother to misbehave in countryside like this with the company of other horses so the riders can really relax and enjoy themselves.*

ABOVE: *When traveling slowly it is fine to sit down in the saddle and will not in any way hinder the horse.*

LEFT: *Once in a canter, the horse will benefit greatly from the weight being eased off his back. It isn't necessary to exaggerate this change in position — with a Western saddle it's impossible anyway. This rider from the USA on her Arab has got it just right and her horse looks very keen and confident in his work. By not slouching, the rider will not tire quickly, so this partnership looks to have quite a few miles of cantering left.*

RIDING OUT

Not all riding out means walking. If the terrain is good, then it may be possible to trot or canter over long distances. This is when rising trot (posting) comes into its own as it spares the horse's back. Remember to change diagonals.

At canter, use the forward seat in open country and sit down if you have to do any dodging about. This may be necessary when riding through trees or along a twisty path when the canter has to remain steady. Again, encourage the horse to work rhythmically. Holding back unnecessarily and accelerating to catch up again will spoil the rhythm and is more likely to agitate the horse and make him difficult to manage.

Horses riding the same route on a regular basis will know all the best places to canter and probably won't wait to be told. They also know when to stop. Should you feel out of control, then take comfort from the fact the horse will either stop from habit or because he is tired and does not want to canter any more. Going home is nearly always quicker than going out, so if you don't enjoy riding at speed, avoid cantering on the second half of the trip.

Riding under overhanging branches does mean that you can't sit bolt upright in the saddle. The safest position to adopt is down to the side of the horse's neck, so that your cheek is almost against his skin. Looking ahead, try to keep your hands and legs in the normal position so that you are still under control. Sit up when it is safe, and only go forward and down as far as is necessary.

RIGHT: *Again, these riders have a long distance to cover, so are not overdoing the forward seat. The rider in front looks to be having a particularly good ride — her horse is keen but controlled, they are in good balance and she is looking where she is going, not down her horse's ears. The second rider is less comfortable — perhaps the horse is not happy going behind. If both horses want to go first, then taking turns is the only way to solve the dilemma. A lead horse held back for too long will tense up and become difficult.*

RESTING AND TYING UP

A long ride does mean that you and the horse will need a break. Having dismounted, run up your stirrups and loosen the girth. Take the reins over the horse's head and undo the noseband. This will then need tucking out of the way, behind his ears, with the loose ends pushed under the rest of the bridle. Let the horse drink straight away unless he is very out of breath. After a drink he can get on with eating the grass or whatever is provided. If there is time to take the saddle off, give his back a good rub down and remove the marks left by the saddle. This can be done with a brush if you have one, washing, or if nothing else, rubbing with your hands. Allowing the horse to get down for a roll is very pleasant for him, as long as you can keep the reins from tangling in his legs and the bridle from being rubbed over his ears.

Taking the bridle off in open countryside is very risky unless you have a headcollar underneath it. If you do have a headcollar, take the bridle off, clean the bit and sponge round the horse's mouth. He will enjoy rinsing his mouth out in clean water given the opportunity and will feel much fresher for it. Check him over for any cuts, bruises, swellings or sores before you tack up again. If you are stiff, tired or sore, then take the opportunity of a stop to change horses with another rider. A different saddle and a fresh horse's way of moving will give you a new start and you will be able to ride in comfort that little bit longer. Alternatively, leading the horse and walking on foot will help you loosen up.

The accepted English method for tying a horse is to use a rope or lead rein which is not attached to the horse's mouth. This is knotted for a quick release in case of emergency, which also means that the knot will not tighten on itself if the horse pulls back. Using the reins to tie a horse can lead to a broken bridle and a bruised mouth. A horse well trained to the Western method will not need tying up so take advice from the people who know the horse before attempting to tie it up at all. Never tie a horse to a moveable object; if the horse moves he will feel he is being chased by what he is tied to and could panic.

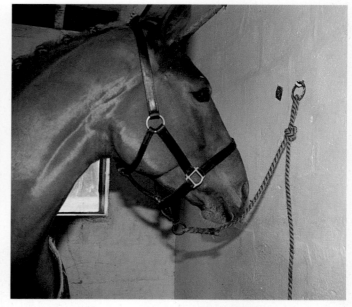

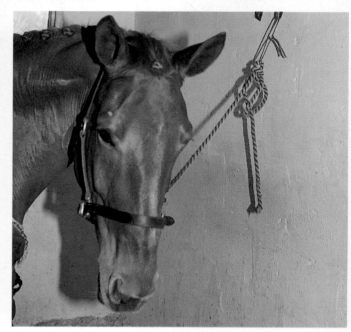

MORE ADVANCED JUMPING

If you have enjoyed jumping so far and wish to take it a bit more seriously, then it is necessary to have a closer look at the various stages of a single jump. Each stage, when ridden well, goes towards making a fluent and successful performance, with both horse and rider confident, safe and enjoying themselves. If any one stage is poorly performed then the whole thing will be spoilt.

The approach describes how you ride towards a fence. Whatever the type of obstacle, the horse should be working 'between leg and hand'. This means the rider is using his legs to create impulsion, rather like using the accelerator in a car, yet containing it with his hands so as not to lose this impulsion. Without fighting, the horse should feel that he could be released into going faster or, in this case, to make a jump. At the same time, a straight line is essential. A wavering approach leads to refusals.

The take-off is the point at which the horse leaves the ground. This is usually the height of the fence away from the fence or half as much again. So if a fence is 1m high, the take off point will be 1-1½m from the base. The shape and type of fence will affect the ideal take-off point and will in turn affect the type of approach.

This sequence of pictures shows the progression to and over a jump. Left to right: holding back to find the right stride, measuring the take-off, full stretch for both horse and rider, coming down to land (horse lands on one foot), readjusting to the first forward stride.

Notice how the rider changes position in order to maintain good balance with the horse as the sequence progresses.

Whilst airborne, the horse's back is rounded, head and neck extended, and his joints well flexed to draw his feet up. The rider's task is to allow him the freedom to do this.

On landing, all the horse's weight is taken for a moment on one foreleg. The point of landing from a good jump will mirror the point of take off. If the rider has just flown out of the saddle, the impact of landing will be many times greater than if he had maintained his balance. The rider, at this point, should be returning to a more up-right posture.

Ride on after landing and look for the next fence. Loss of control on and after landing can be tricky to regain and leaves the horse free to think of something quite irrelevant to the job in hand. He may, for instance, be attracted by a group of waiting horses and so leave the chosen line of approach for the next fence.

LEFT: *Getting the right line to a fence means thinking well ahead. Before landing from one fence, an experienced rider will already be looking ahead for the next. If the jump is of a reasonable size, so that the horse is off the ground for long enough, this will bring about a sufficient change of balance to influence the horse's landing. This partnership (Joe Fergis on 'Mill Pearl' USA) are of one mind – they both know exactly where they are going so have every chance of completing a successful round.*

RIGHT: *These two pictures show a very extreme example of being left behind. They suggest a breakdown in communication somewhere, which has got the horse taking off when the rider was not expecting it. Even so, she has made a strenuous effort to leave the horse's head free and he still jumps with amazingly good style. Had she not slipped the reins, she would undoubtedly have brought the horse crashing down on to the fence.*

Cross-country jumping requires much quick-thinking, agility and courage from both horse and rider and a certain amount of jumping to higher or lower ground. Consequently, this kind of picture is more likely to occur than in show-jumping, where great technical accuracy is more important than bravado.

Getting the 'line' right requires practice and is best done by using easy fences. These can be raised or made more difficult once a flowing performance is established. If you do make a mistake which perhaps brings you to a jump at an awkward angle, then you are less likely to have a stop or to knock the fence down. Building a course of jumps is an art in itself, but broadly speaking, try to make the turns from one jump to the next with wide angles and plenty of room to put things right if necessary. Circling between jumps is a good idea unless you are actually riding in a competition, in which case it counts as a refusal.

Never ride to a fence unless you feel that you and the horse are both going well. If you have been standing around, even for a few minutes, do some circle work to warm up the horse and get his attention. This is best done so that the edge of your circle keeps touching the approach line. In this way, when the moment is right, open out the circle on to the approach line and away you go.

An over-enthusiastic horse will need settling first using either walk or trot. He will probably pick up a few canter strides before take-off of his own volition and then need quietly settling again afterwards. Although jumping at great speed can be exciting, it is much more difficult to judge the take-off point successfully without the necessary thinking time.

A slower horse will need waking up before the final approach. Without the necessary impulsion he may slow down and either stop altogether or get too close to the fence before taking off. Such a horse needs riding forward with great determination, particularly on the last two or three strides.

Timing is something which requires skill, and this will come with experience. This is what sets the great riders apart from the ordinary. An impeccable sense of timing can make up for a lack of style, as can be seen with a number of international show jumpers. The point at which a horse takes off will make a great difference to the feel of the jump from the rider's point of view. Taking off too close makes more of a buck jump, which can be unseating. This is one reason why a nervous rider shouldn't be pushed into jumping too big a fence. Without the commitment to ride into a jump, a close take-off is much more likely to happen. Taking off too far back, or too early, means the horse flattens out and runs the risk of not getting enough height. This is more comfortable for the rider as long as he is not caught unawares, thus getting 'left behind'.

Getting into forward seat on the approach takes some of the necessity out of knowing exactly when the horse will take off. You will be in a safe position already. Being left behind means sitting up and falling back on the horse's mouth just at the point he needs to stretch his head and neck out.

A rider in the forward seat will not interfere at this point. His hands should be quiet and still, not restricting by being too tight. It is not necessary to throw your arms forward and you may feel happier holding on to a piece of mane. Flinging your arms around will distract the horse and he will be more likely to jump hollow – head up, back hollow, legs trailing. This is uncomfortable for both horse and rider and potentially dangerous. The same result will come about if the rider has his reins too short and too tight to allow the horse freedom in his head and neck.

At the point of landing the rider should be looking up ready to ride forward as the horse picks up his first few strides. You may have to ride a circle to calm him down, or encourage him forward with your legs; the horse should continue working, so that he doesn't lose his concentration.

BELOW: *Eddie Macken (Ireland), riding 'Welfenkrone' who picks his feet up well in front and can be seen here at full stretch for the mid-point of the jump.*

RIGHT: *Anne Kursiniski and 'Starman' (USA) showing classic style.*

OVERLEAF: *The same can be said for Janet Hunter and 'Everest Lisnamarrow' (see page 101). Haute Luther and 'Nolis de Thurin' from Germany (page 100) demonstrate how to ride down a steel bank in style at Hickstead Derby.*

REFUSALS

Sooner or later, the horse you are riding is going to refuse or 'run out' (dodge past the jump). Before you attempt to rectify the situation you must ask yourself why this has happened. Running out is nearly always due to a bad approach unless something has frightened the horse at the last moment. Refusing is a different matter — there are almost countless reasons for it. The question is, why?

Fear, pain, cowardice, ignorance and poor riding cover most possibilities. If you, or a previous rider have pulled the horse in the mouth over a jump already, he will not be too keen to repeat the experience. Firm riding and reassurance will encourage him to try again, and then it is up to you to make sure you do not put him off a second time. Some horses simply do not like jumping. Repeated punishment from learner riders can contribute to this, or lack of agility on the horse's part.

'Overfacing' is a definite discouragement. Asking a horse to jump something beyond his capability or training is unfair. If this is the case, lowering the jump or making it more inviting will help him to regain his confidence. Sometimes, it is necessary to go right back to a pole on the ground, and then build the fence up by degrees. A tired horse can be overfaced by something he would normally tackle with ease.

Pain can be caused by ill-fitting saddlery, bad shoeing, poor riding, knocking a fence, or a fall. If a horse is lame, it may not be evident until he is asked to jump, and then the impact of landing will be uncomfortable. This is usually worse when the ground is hard.

A young or inexperienced horse will refuse if faced with a type of obstacle he is not used to. Some horses are happy to have a go at any obstacle while others are very suspicious of anything new. Taking a lead from an older horse, provided the jump is not too big, is often enough to give the youngster confidence. Otherwise, allowing him to take a closer look before being asked to jump, will have the same result.

There are very few occasions when using a whip is beneficial. If you can be absolutely certain that your approach was perfect, that the horse has no good reason to stop except laziness, then perhaps it will work. If you are wrong, then hitting him will ultimately make him worse not better, and who can blame him? The whip is intended only to reinforce the leg aids, not to punish, so should only be used sparingly at any time.

To help both horse and rider to judge the take-off point, ground lines and placing poles can be a great help. A ground line is a pole placed

LEFT, TOP AND BOTTOM
Repeated refusals demand some kind of action and this pony could well be overfaced. To have practically fallen off twice suggests that the rider tackled the approach with some gusto, so enthusiasm alone has proved insufficient. Lowering the fences would certainly help. Some young horses feel happier with natural-looking jumps, and having gained experience over them are then more willing to tackle colored jumps such as these.

BELOW: *Jumping a spread fence encourages the horse to stretch and round his topline. This horse is using his head and neck really well because the rider is not restricting him either with her hands or by not going forward enough.*

BELOW RIGHT: *David Broome demonstrating delicate, stylish and effective use of the hands. The rein is taut with a light contact (look at the bit resting in the corners of the horse's mouth) and the classic straight line from his elbow to the bit rings.*

immediately in front of the jump, secured so that it cannot be rolled. This can prevent the horse taking off too close and will make it easier for him to judge the height of the fence. A ground line on the opposite (landing) side has the opposite effect and is off-putting. Placing poles are used to correct the striding before take off. Wrongly placed poles will create problems, so this is best left to an experienced rider or trainer. All horses have different lengths of stride which vary according to their way of going. Although it is possible to give guidelines as to distances, these can only be approximate. If they don't suit a particular horse, they are not much help.

A fence with too big a gap between the poles is not inviting. Fillers such as brushwood, or crosspoles can fill in these gaps to make a jump more appealing. Natural looking fences, called 'rustics', are always more inviting than the bright obstacles used in show jumping.

COMPLEX JUMPS

If two or more jumps are placed so that the horse has room for only one or two strides between them, they are known as combinations, two jumps making a double and three, a treble. They are more difficult to tackle than single fences. A mistake made at the first element means that jumping the second will be worse, so it is important to meet the first part of a combination exactly right. However, a very low jump placed one carefully measured canter stride in front of a bigger jump will have the effect of 'putting the horse right', so that the second element then becomes easier. Generally, jumping combinations is a progressive move to be made when success has been achieved over a variety of single fences. A jumping lane, using three or more fences in combination is a useful aid to improving both horse and rider's agility, timing, and balance.

A jump which has width as well as height is called a spread. If there are two rails at the same height — the highest point — it is a parallel. Spread fences are the easiest for a horse to judge and the most encouraging if the highest rail is also the furthest from take-off. Jumping a spread back to front is actually dangerous, so always make sure that the jump you approach is ascending away from you, however small it is. Parallels demand more accurate riding so should be left until you are quite confident and successful with simple uprights and spreads.

LEFT: *Riding with a safe hat is always a wise move, more especially when you have no idea beforehand what kind of horses you will be expected to ride (see previous pages). The second and third horses here look big and bright, which is fun for a capable rider but not really relaxing for a novice. At least if your head is protected you know you have lessened your chances of a severe accident should anything go wrong.*

RIDING HOLIDAYS

For the novice rider, venturing out on your first riding holiday can be very exciting. Barring accidents, all that extra time spent in the saddle will give you valuable experience and should leave you with extra confidence in your abilities. Choosing a good riding holiday is often a matter of chance as you are unlikely to be able to do a tour of inspection before you book up. It is always possible to make a few basic checks, though, to be sure you are not over-stretching yourself.

Find out what level of riding is catered for. If the brochure says the holiday is for experienced riders only, then you should at least be capable of riding at speed and over a few jumps. You will probably need to be quite fit, too. Check on the number of hours you will be expected to spend riding each day and should this sound excessive, if you will be able to drop out at any stage if it does prove too much. Make sure your height and weight is suitable for the horses and ponies to be used.

Riding holidays can vary from intensive courses of training for the real enthusiast to providing a means of enjoying otherwise inaccessible countryside. It could involve riding out on a different route every day from the riding center or using the horse as a means of transport. The latter often requires some knowledge of horse care if you are camping overnight. Getting your own horse ready for your lessons at home, and settling him back in his stable afterwards is a useful way to rehearse for this, unless you have a friend with a horse you can practise on. If you enjoy riding then you will probably enjoy looking after the horse you ride anyway.

There are few places in the world which don't cater for riding holidays in some form or another.

Riding native ponies or horses in their own territory is particularly rewarding and exciting. For example, Iceland has one breed only of small but amazingly strong and sure-footed ponies which will carry you across some of the most thrilling landscape in the world. The British Isles have nine native breeds, the best riding country being in the home of the Highland ponies of Scotland, the Fells and Dales in northern England, the Welsh ponies of Wales and the ancient Exmoor breed in the West Country. In the United States of America, trail rides are a speciality and will give you a taste of the Old West.

One thing about being on horseback which you will soon discover, is that other wild creatures are often less afraid of man in the presence of a horse. Riding on safari in parts of Africa is increasingly popular, but you need to be fit for this kind of activity. For a completely new riding experience, it is possible to ride across the Steppes of Mongolia. Mongolian ponies have a rather wild temperament and are ridden with wooden saddles, which can take a bit of getting used to!

Although one cannot expect to find the same standards of safety in the remoter parts of the world, it is still wise to take as many precautions as possible wherever you ride. If you think you may get a chance to ride at your chosen destination, at least pack some safe footwear which may double for walking as well.

Once you have learnt to ride, you will never completely forget the rudiments even if you don't ride again for several years. Riding is fun, challenging and rewarding. As an introduction to horse riding, I hope this book has whetted your appetite for more and that your life to come will be enriched by your acquaintance with horses.

ABOVE: *Competing in the Golden Horseshoe Final, Exmoor. Long-distance riding or trail riding, is not for the faint-hearted. To qualify for this Exmoor final, the competitors will have ridden 40 miles at an average speed equating to a fast trot. The final itself totals 75 miles over two days, so it's no wonder this pair are enjoying a relaxing walk. Before even considering riding long distances on holiday you would need to be extremely fit and used to long hours in the saddle.*

RIGHT: *Touring the countryside on horseback gives you an opportunity to see the area from quite a different viewpoint. For one thing, you will be able to cover a much wider area than you could on foot, and you will have access to places inaccessible to motor transport. Riding is very much what you want it to be. Having enjoyed several miles of relaxing walking, perhaps you'll need a sharp canter to get the adrenalin flowing.*

Glossary

Aids   Means of conveying rider's wishes to horse. Artificial aids include whips, spurs and martingales.
Natural aids are voice, hands, seat, legs, body and weight.

Arnica   Homeopathic remedy for strains and bruises.

Bascule   The shape a horse makes when jumping. Good bascule comes from the freedom to be allowed to jump without interference from the rider – back rounded, head and neck extended forward and down, joints well flexed under the body.

Bit   Part of bridle which goes in the horse's mouth. Made from a variety of different materials, but is usually metal.

Break pace   Horse changes gait unintentionally, eg. trotting a few steps having lost rhythm in canter, or jogs when should be walking.

Bridging the reins   The spare end of each rein is taken in the opposite hand to make a bridge over the horse's withers. The rider is therefore able to lean on the bridge for balance without interfering with the horse's mouth or losing the capacity to use the reins for control. A technique used extensively in racing.

Cantle   Back of saddle.

Changing rein   Changing direction. The left rein is anti-clockwise (for left-handed turns), the right is clockwise.

Cross-country   Riding out in the countryside. Also a phase of horse trials (one, two and three-day eventing) which involves jumping a series of natural (rustic) fences, including ditches, hedges, post and rails, and water.

Diagonal   Near-fore and off-hind legs together (left diagonal) or off-fore and near-hind together (right diagonal). A horse moves in diagonals when trotting.

Disunited   In canter, horses occasionally change lead behind so that the canter becomes disjointed and incorrect in sequence. Instead of a diagonal pair of legs marking the second beat of a stride, a lateral pair is used.

Double   Two jumps only one or two canter strides apart.

Double bridle   Bridle with two bits with differing actions. Used mainly for dressage and showing or for strong horses which are difficult to manage with a milder bit. Should only be used by skilled riders when its action should not be severe. Roughly used, a double bridle is severe.

Dressage   Training of the horse. A separate phase in Horse Trials performed in a marked-out arena without jumps, measuring either 20m × 40m or 20 × 60m. Dressage is very demanding on the mental and physical concentration of both horse and rider.

Flying change   Change of leading leg in canter without either walking, trotting or halting. Only a well-trained horse will be able to do this successfully.

Impulsion   Horse's desire to go forward, hence a horse can have impulsion in halt as well as the four gaits or while reining back.

Irons   Stirrup irons. That part of the stirrups which supports the rider's feet.

Jodhpurs   Riding trousers with reinforced inside knee patches.

Lame   Description of horse limping. Limping is not a term used in horsey parlance.

ABOVE: *It is important to check that the girth is tight enough – a loose saddle could be very dangerous.*

RIGHT: *An indoor lesson with a small group can be very rewarding as pupils learn from each other.*

Lungeing	Working a horse on a circle from the ground, the trainer marking the center of the circle. Involves use of a lunge rein, whip and cavesson. A lunge cavesson fits over the bridle, a lunge rein is attached to this, the other end being held by the trainer. A lunge whip is used to help control the horse's position and forward movement.
Make much	Reward the horse with a pat.
Martingale	Attachment to bridle to improve control of the horse. Martingales are often referred to as gadgets and are frowned upon by purists. Types in common use are:
	i) Running martingale. Comes between horse's front legs from the girth and then divides in two. These two straps have metal rings at the end through which run the reins. Held in place by a neckstrap.
	ii) Standing martingale. Comes from the girth, through the neckstrap as the running martingale. Single strap then loops on to a simple (cavesson) noseband.
	iii) Irish martingale. A single short piece of leather with small ring at each end. The reins go through these rings, so the martingale is suspended under the horse's neck. Prevents the reins being flipped over the horse's head if it should toss head sideways.
Napping	Disinclination to go forwards particularly away from home and other horses.
Neckstrap	Strap placed round horse's neck, resting against the shoulders. Normally part of a martingale, a neckstrap can provide a useful handhold for learner riders.
On the bit	Expression used to describe the way a horse works, whereby he is accepting the rider's aids without resistance. He will be active and willing and show some degree of 'arching' in his neck, the amount varying according to his level of training. This arching is usually described as flexion.
Pace	Pacing is working in laterals, two legs on the same side moving together. 'Pace' is frequently used to refer to the gaits.
Pommel	Front arch of saddle.
Posting	Rising trot.
Quick release knot	Means of tying a horse to a solid object so that the knot can be undone with a single tug.
Rearing	A vice whereby the horse stands up on his hindlegs to resist going forwards.
Rising trot	Posting.
Running out	Dodging past a jump. Technically a refusal.
Seat	Rider's posterior. Also part of saddle.
Side reins	Used during lunging. Two straps running from the bit to the girth or saddle, one on each side.
Shying	If a horse is startled and jumps sideways unexpectedly, this is called shying.
Tit-bits	Hand-fed items of food used for reward. Apples, carrots, etc are most suitable but should be cut lengthwise to avoid choking. Most horses are partial to non-sticky mints.
Transition	Change from one gait to another.
Treble	Three fences in a line, only one or two strides apart.
Wrong-leg (lead)	Incorrect lead in canter.

INDEX

aggression 25
aids 338, 39, 40

behavior 20, 20, 22
blind spots 21
Broome, David 103
bucking and rearing 80, 80, 81
   napping 80

Camargue, the 25
cantering 44, 52, 52, 91
Caspian pony 15
class size 15
cleanliness 14
clothing
   footwear 16
   gloves 16
   hat 16, 17
   jodhpurs 16
   protective 16, 16
competitive riding 41
cross country 86, 86, 89, 90
   jumping 96

discipline 15
dismounting 38, 38
dressage 11, 12, 72
drinking 22

equipment 31
exercises 60, 61, 66
   arm folding 63
   back, waist and chest 62
   seat and legs 64-66, 65
   shoulders and arms 61-62, 62, 63
   stretching 62-63, 63
Exmoor breed 106

falling off 82, 82
Fells and Dales in northern England
106
Fergis, Joe 96
food 23

galloping 44, 76, 76
Golden Horseshoe Ride, Exmoor 89,
106
Green, Lucinda 76
ground feeding 12

hacking out 41, 56, 69-84
herd hierarchy 23
Hickstead 12
   Derby 98
Highland ponies, Scotland 106
horses' welfare 11-12
Hunter, Janet 98

indoor lesson 11
indoor riding arena 11

jockey skull hats 17
jumping 70, 70, 71, 72, 74, 74, 75, 102
   advanced 94, 94, 96, 96
   buck 98
   complex 102
   position 70
   timing 98

knee gripping 72
Kursiniski, Anne 98

leading 30, 30, 31
long-distance or trail riding 106
Loriston-Clarke, Jenny 12
lunge lessons 56, 57, 60, 60, 64
Lusitano horses, Portugal 12, 17
Luther, Haute 98

Macken, Eddie 98
misbehavior 80
modern hunting seat 70, 71
moods 25
mounting 36, 36, 38
movement 42-54
moving off 39-41

New Zealand rug 15

overfacing 102

pole work 75, 76
Pony Club 41
   hunter trial 16
posture 41, 60, 60, 63, 64, 72, 72

Quarter Horse 32
quick release knot 12, 92

refusal 80, 102, 102
reins 38, 38, 39
   bridging 76
resting 92, 92
riding holidays 10, 106, 107
riding out 11, 91, 91
riding schools 10-19

saddles 32, 39
   Australian stock 34
   dressage 32, 34, 72
   event 32
   flat pony 32
   general purpose 34
   jumping 32
   race exercise 34
   show 32, 34
   side 34

safari, riding on 106
safety 11, 106
seat 60
sensitivity 20
snack feeding 26-27, 27
spacing 89
spread fence 103, 103
steering 40
stirrup leathers 32, 34, 36

tack, cleaning 32
technical improvement 56, 56
trekking 88
trotting 41, 44, 45, 46, 47-50, 66
   rising trot 44, 47, 48, 50, 50, 91
tying up 92, 92

understanding horses 20-29
USA 106

walking 41, 41, 44, 45
Welsh ponies 106
Western style 32, 47, 90

Acknowledgments

The author and publisher would like to thank the following for their help in the preparation of this book: Adrian Hodgkins the designer, Helen Dawson for the index, Nicki Giles for production and Judith Millidge the editor.

We are also grateful to Kit Houghton Photography for supplying all the illustrations except the small one on page 60.

The author and publisher would like to stress that this book is intended only as a guide to basic equestrianism, and is no substitute for a course of lessons from a professional riding school.